Lessons from
Cross-Cultural Collaboration

Lessons from Cross-Cultural Collaboration

How Cultural Humility Informed and Shaped the Work of an American and a Kenyan

To Katy —

Many blessings —

Eloise Hockett

and

John Muhanji

Eloise Hockett

August 15, 2017

WIPF & STOCK · Eugene, Oregon

LESSONS FROM CROSS-CULTURAL COLLABORATION
How Cultural Humility Informed and Shaped the Work of an American and a Kenyan

Wipf & Stock
An Imprint of Wipf and Stock Publishers
199 W. 8th Ave., Suite 3
Eugene, OR 97401

www.wipfandstock.com

PAPERBACK ISBN: 978-1-5326-0915-2
HARDCOVER ISBN: 978-1-5326-0917-6
EBOOK ISBN: 978-1-5326-0916-9

Manufactured in the U.S.A.   APRIL 10, 2017

Contents

Preface

ELOISE AND JOHN ARE not really certain when they first started talking or thinking about writing a book describing their cross-cultural work in Kenya, but Eloise believes John gets the credit for first verbalizing the idea that he and Eloise should write a book. John's initial comment may have been somewhat of a joke or passing comment in jest at the time, but somehow that initial comment remained in the back of their minds for quite a while, until early 2016.

As Eloise and John's collaborative work in Kenya increased, Eloise always took copious notes so she and John could discuss what had taken place and what it all meant. She would pepper John with unending clarifying questions in order to understand the culture and significance with specific events and interactions. Some of their projects also became a part of Eloise's research plan as a part of her role as a university professor. Eloise would write up many of her and John's experiences and then share with friends, families, and supporters along the way. Some of those writings also became published articles in other sources. The more information Eloise shared with people, the more others began to suggest the idea of writing a book of her and John's experiences.

One cold and wintry Saturday morning while on a long walk, Eloise was thinking about her writing projects and how best to organize them in order to get them ready for publication in selected sources. All of a sudden, it seemed like everything fell into place, and Eloise believes God gave her a clear outline for the concept of this book that very morning. She proceeded home as fast as possible, ran to her computer, and wrote up the conceptual outline. Then she immediately emailed John the outline for his approval and asked him if he was "in" for real on this book project. She also told him that she was not going to proceed to write a book without him since the entire concept was based on their collaborative work. John did not hesitate to say yes to this new collaborative effort!

Eloise and John had already collaborated on writing a few smaller articles, in addition to preparing presentations for speaking engagements, so they were used to the process of collaborating from a long distance and decided to use Google Docs once again for this endeavor. As the book began to take shape, many discussions ensued through almost every communication medium possible. Since John was in Kenya and Eloise in Oregon, regular communication with updates were necessary for forward progress and meeting specific goals for completion. The invitation to publish with Wipf and Stock came while Eloise was in Kenya at Kaptama hospital with yet another team of nursing students. It was a joy to share that news with John in real time and in the same location. Before Eloise left Kenya at the conclusion of that trip just a few days later, she and John had already mapped out the final details for completing this book, each one adding their unique strengths and abilities to the process.

However, in spite of a well-organized plan, this completion did not come without a number of challenges. As Eloise and John neared the finish line, it seemed that more interruptions and discouragements than normal came their way both personally and professionally. However, both Eloise and John have pressed on toward the goal, believing that God has continued to sustain them in order to share their stories of cross-cultural collaboration with a broader audience.

As Eloise and John have written and edited the content of this book, they have once again been reminded of God's leading and direction through each aspect of their collaborative work. None of the projects they have worked on together could have been started and carried out without God's divine guidance, along with the ongoing support of other partners along the way.

The premise of this book is based on the concept of cultural humility and how Eloise and John have used the foundational components of cultural humility within their various cross-cultural collaborative initiatives. As they describe each project, they make the necessary connections to cultural humility and share specific insights and key learning from each experience. In addition, Eloise has incorporated some of her research findings throughout the content.

Eloise and John hope and pray that the content of this book will be a source of inspiration to others as to how God is indeed still working throughout the world. It is not necessary for us to bring God to other parts of the world since he has been in the world from the beginning of time. Rather, God invites each one of us to be his hands and feet and partner with him throughout the world as he leads us to engage with others in ministry of all kinds whether locally or globally. It is the responsibility of each person to be open to God's leading and discern how God desires to use us in each situation. As Eloise and John continue to discover in their collaborative work, when people partner together in respectful and meaningful ways which honors the culture and diversity of others, God uses those efforts to further his work in the world. Each of us, working with others through God's direction and leading, can indeed make a difference in our world.

John and Eloise invite you, the reader, to journey with them in the stories of their cross-cultural collaboration in Kenya.

Acknowledgments

ALTHOUGH THERE ARE MANY people we could thank for assisting us in this work, trying to list all of them would surely leave someone out. The following acknowledgments include those who have made the most impact through our lives and have helped to shape our work.

From Eloise

To husband Steve: You have fully supported me through two advanced degrees and now this book. I am most grateful for your love and support for all of the projects I am involved with in Kenya, and yet again as I took on another project. You continue to be a vital part of this important work as you keep friends and family informed as I am away, in addition to keeping things in order at home. This truly is a partnership in so many ways, as you affirm God's calling for the ministry in Kenya.

To my colleagues Linda Samek and Scot Headley: Your support of this Kenya work from the beginning of the peace curriculum has been instrumental in moving these projects forward. When we first discussed the concept of cultural humility and wrote our first article on it, I do not believe any of us knew at the time how God would continue to use and shape these concepts in all aspects of our work.

To my colleague Terry Huffman: Thank-you for encouraging me to pursue this book idea and for your ongoing support as I shared my progress. Over the years you have willingly provided key professional advice over cups of coffee. I am grateful for your mentorship in my research through the years.

To my friend Gregg Lamm: Not too long into my involvement in Kenya, you brought a word to me before I left for one of my trips. You pulled me aside after church one day and said: "Eloise, I want you to be fluid." It was a very simple message, yet one that has continued to shape my work in so many ways, not only in Kenya, but also in my teaching and leading. I believe God gave you that message to share with me for a very specific reason.

To John: Thank-you for your countless hours of discussions and patiently answering all of my never-ending questions. I have learned so much from our collaboration over the years. You continue to stretch and challenge me in so many ways personally and professionally. It is a privilege and honor to call you friend.

From John

To my wife Rose: I appreciate your never-ending support for this important work here in Kenya. Without such a woman as you by my side, I could not accomplish all that I have been able to do. You are truly my partner and my rock.

To my children, Kevin, Audrey, and Allan: I am blessed to have such wonderful children who are not only the light of my life, but who encourage me to keep going with the work God has called me to do. It is a joy to watch you continue growing in God's goodness and grace.

In honor of my late father and mother: Both were instrumental in my upbringing as they modeled constant dedication and service to Christ and his work. I truly am the man I am today because of my parent's example, love, and prayers on my life.

Introduction

WHY WOULD AN AMERICAN educator and a Kenyan ministry director pursue writing a book together about cross-cultural collaboration? What do these professionals have to offer that would be of value and inspiration to others who are involved in cross-cultural efforts around the world? Those are very good questions, and ones the authors hope to answer in this introduction and subsequently throughout the entire book.

Eloise Hockett, an American and tenured professor at George Fox University, has a passion for education and justice related issues, especially for women and girls in Kenya. John Muhanji, is a Kenyan and a former banker in Kenya, and currently Director, Africa Ministries Office for Friends United Meeting (FUM), an American based Quaker organization. John has a passion for evangelism, leadership development in the Quaker churches, promoting justice for the oppressed, and meeting the needs of his own people, in addition to others in Africa and beyond.

Eloise and John's story of cross-cultural collaboration began in 2008 when John contacted Eloise's institution, George Fox University, for assistance in writing a peace curriculum for the Quaker schools in Kenya. Eloise was invited to join the George Fox education team that explored this invitation and discerned how, or if, to proceed. As God continued to open doors to participate with this important project, Eloise was on the first and subsequent teams which went to Kenya in 2009 to collaborate with the Kenyans on the peace curriculum project. After only a few visits to Kenya engaging in the peace curriculum project, it was clearly evident to Eloise and her colleagues that this initial project was just the impetus of future collaborative work with the Quakers in Kenya. In his role as Africa

Ministries Director for Friends United Meeting, John was the point person from the start and continued to be Eloise's main contact for the initial peace curriculum project, and all of the projects that have followed. Through their years of working together, John and Eloise have discovered that while their skills and abilities are distinctly different, those skills and abilities when brought together, complement each other, especially in their collaborative ministry efforts in Kenya and also with their speaking and writing projects.

While there are already many publications addressing effective cross-cultural collaboration and international work or initiatives, the authors believe this book is unique, in that, they describe their collaborative ministry work which represents two professionals coming from totally different backgrounds and perspectives. The key ideas for this book are framed around the educational and ministry work Eloise and John have already completed or are currently involved with in Kenya. Further, the story of each specific project is framed through the lens of a newer approach of cross-cultural collaboration, that of cultural humility. Eloise and John believe that their combined voices and stories from the viewpoints of an American and a Kenyan lend to the strength of the various tenets of cultural humility, and how those tenets have informed their practice within their cross-cultural collaboration work, as well as within their own cultures. Through Eloise and John's years of working together, their goal has been to model the principles of cultural humility as best as possible in their professional interactions by honoring the other person's views and ideas, respecting each other, listening to each other, learning from one another, and building trust with each other.

The first chapter of this book explains the concept of cultural humility by providing definitions and examples for each one of the main tenets or themes. Each subsequent chapter then fully describes Eloise and John's key projects in Kenya, the perspectives of each project, key lessons learned, and any appropriate applications. In addition, specific connections to cultural humility are woven throughout each chapter.

As Eloise and John share the insights of their work, they also incorporate the lens of reflective practice, whereby one further assesses personal motives, assumptions, and outcomes of the work, which can then lead to further growth and development as a professional.[1] Through this reflective process, Eloise and John identify the successes and challenges for each

1. Larivee, Transforming Teaching Practice, 294; Osterman and Kottman, *Reflective Practice for Educators*, 2–3.

project, and conclude with practical advice they would have for others who are engaging in cross-cultural initiatives whether locally or globally.

Even though Eloise and John will be writing about the various projects or initiatives they have undertaken together using the principles of cultural humility, they want to make it known that their collaborative work in Kenya is just not their work alone. Countless other people have participated in the work alongside Eloise and John, but unfortunately it is not possible to list them all. When it is important to the narrative to name key participants, Eloise and John will do so because of specific contributions to that particular project.

It is Eloise and John's prayer and goal that within the work they do, they will continue to involve and engage others so that they too can have a part in cross-cultural collaboration that respects the diversity of God's kingdom and His people. Eloise and John firmly believe that engaging globally is a must for all people to understand God's diversity in the world and build relationships with people who are different than they are. Even more importantly, through this type of cross-cultural work using the framework of cultural humility, each one of us has the opportunity to engage with God's work and people around the world in settings which are not the norm for us.

With the continued support of their families and friends, Eloise and John do not see an end to the ministry opportunities God has called them to do in Africa and other parts of the world. They are looking forward to their continued collaborative work especially in Kenya using the guiding principles of cultural humility.

1

Principles of Cultural Humility

RELATIONSHIPS WITH OTHERS ARE a core element of our existence as human beings. God created us first to be in relationship with him, then to have relationships with others. Building strong and healthy relationships does not often come naturally, and it takes intentional efforts to make them work. Even with the best of intentions, we may fail at building relationships with others for many reasons. Relationships can bring both joy or sorrow to our lives, but no matter the difficulties, we still need to carry out God's plan for all of us to be in relationship with one another.

While building relationships with those who are like us might be easier to form, building relationships with those who represent different nationalities and cultures can present challenges all their own. God created each one of us, and therefore we all bear the image of God and his diversity. With the world changing as it is, with many more opportunities to interact with those from other cultural backgrounds and experiences, we especially need to learn how to relate to anyone we come in contact with. It is vitally important now more than ever before to recognize the various ways, positively or negatively, in which we interact and engage with those who are different than we are, thus demonstrating appreciation for cross-cultural diversity while recognizing it is God's intention for such diversity and collaboration.

Opportunities to engage with others and build relationships do not occur just in global settings, but also locally in our communities, churches, schools, or wherever people work or play together. Cultural differences may occur even within the same organizations, sometimes to a great degree. With so much emphasis on cultural issues in any setting, the questions remain: Why should we pay attention to the ways in which we interact with others? Why is it so difficult for many of us to engage with others in a positive way? Finally, what is so important about healthy and positive interactions with those from other cultures that embody how Jesus interacted with all people throughout his ministry?

It is commonly understood that each of us has our own lens of how we view the world. This lens has developed from childhood on and is informed by our own culture based on where we live (or have lived) and work, and our family upbringing.[1] Often it is difficult to change our way of thinking and interacting when we have been so entrenched in one particular way of knowing, thinking, and doing. Most current writing on international and global initiatives and on cross-cultural or mission work contains vocabulary full of words relating to culture and cultural interactions. It is generally assumed that those engaged in cross-cultural work of any kind exhibit some sort of competency related to cultural interactions.

The word *culture* is multifaceted and includes not just language, but all of the related customs, practices, and rules—spoken or unspoken. In general terms, the word *culture* can be defined as: "the customary beliefs, social forms, and material traits of a racial, religious, or social group."[2] In Kroeber and Kluckhohn's work, they identify the main components of culture as:

> . . . patterns, explicit and implicit, of and for behavior acquired and transmitted by symbols, constituting the distinctive achievements of human groups, including their embodiments in artifacts; the essential core of culture consists of traditional (i.e. historically derived and selected) ideas and especially their attached values; culture systems may, on the one hand, be considered as products of action, and on the other as conditioning elements of further action.[3]

According to David Livermore, "Culture shapes the way we think; it alters how and what we learn. Two individuals can receive the same information and their respective cultures can lead them to arrive at two entirely different conclusions."[4] From these foundational definitions emerge many terms related to cultural interactions and behaviors, which are often used interchangeably, but have different meanings. Following are a few

1. Christie et al., "Putting Transformational Learning into Practice," 11.

2. Merriam-Webster.com.

3. Kroeber and Kluckhohn, *Culture: A Critical Review of Concepts*, 47.

4. Livermore, *Serving with Eyes Wide Open*, 78.

definitions of some of the more common culturally related terms that can assist in our understanding of cultural interactions.

Cultural awareness can be described as a general knowledge gained from a variety of sources in which a person may have limited or no experience or emotional ties with those from other cultures.[5]

Cultural competence refers to general knowledge and skills related to cultural groups. This definition primarily assumes some sort of a checklist in which someone has achieved some level of understanding about a particular group of people. The concept of cultural competence can also be limiting, in that the focus tends to be on general knowledge of ethnic groups, instead of a focus on each individual and their needs from that group.[6]

Cultural sensitivity is the ability to carefully and respectfully compare and contrast cultural differences through the lens of one's own cultural experiences and make appropriate responses.[7]

Cultural intelligence describes a person who exhibits a fluid and successful navigation and adaptation of different cultural experiences and settings in such a way that is both natural and respectful of the present culture.[8]

While all of these terms provide some guidance when working with those of other cultures, Eloise and John believe these terms do not go deep enough to inform one's work with other cultures in a healthy and meaningful way no matter if the work is short-term or long-term, locally or internationally based.

Other definitions relating to cultural understanding and interactions have recently emerged in academic and missional work. *Cultural humility* is a newer concept, taking cultural understanding and interactions in a different direction. *Cultural humility,* a term which originated in the health care field, promotes a holistic approach in working with those of other cultures, by taking the focus off oneself and placing it on others.[9] Tervalon and Murray-Garcia were the first to coin the term *cultural humility* within their

---

5. Hardy and Laszlosfly, The Cultural Genogram, 2; Sermeno, Building a Case for Cultural Sensitivity, 11.

6. Chang et al., Integrating Cultural Humility, 271.

7. Hardy and Laszlosfly, The Cultural Genogram, 2.

8. Earley and Ang, *Cultural Intelligence*, 59.

9. Ross, Notes from the Field, 316; Tangney, Humility: Theoretical Perspectives, 72; Tervalon and Murray-Garcia, Cultural Humility Versus Cultural Competence, 121.

profession of social work as a response to mandates for more multicultural training for health care workers. The components of cultural humility provide a loosely held framework or guiding principles which move each of us beyond mere proficiencies or competencies, and place us in the role of a life-long learner regarding culture and interactions with those who are different than we are.[10] The framework of cultural humility also redefines the way we think and interact with those of another culture, leading to more respectful interactions and a better understanding of more appropriate and relevant ways to meet the needs of those with whom we work.[11]

Taking also into consideration a Christian perspective, cultural humility is deeply rooted within the biblical principle of humility found in Philippians 2:3: "in humility count others more significant than yourselves." God himself exhibited the principle of cultural humility through the incarnation of Jesus Christ as revealed in John 3:16: "For God so loved the world that he gave his only Son, so that everyone who believes in him may not perish but may have eternal life." As a result of that incarnation, Jesus carried through the concept of cultural humility during his entire ministry. Jesus washed the feet of his disciples, surrounded himself with needy people, and spoke to women, in addition to setting other examples that demonstrated cultural humility. However, for many Christians, and non-Christians as well, humility can be the hardest attribute to develop, since is counter to human nature. Chang, Simon, and Dong note that the development of humility is ongoing.[12] Eloise and John would argue that it is a lifelong process without a conclusion on this earth. Duane Elmer notes that "Humility is a lifestyle, not isolated incidents. It is an attitude toward God, ourselves and others that permeates our thoughts and deeds."[13] Further, humility also requires that we shed our pride and become one who receives from others, not one who only gives to others. Humility is a form of sacrifice, in that we sacrifice our own needs, comforts, ambitions, and desires in order to meet the needs of others.

Those who call themselves followers of Christ especially have the responsibility to put others first with humility in true servanthood. As noted by Chang, Simon, and Dong, humility begins by examining one's own

---

10. Hook, Engaging Clients with Cultural Humility, 278.

11. Hockett et al., Cultural Humility, 26.

12. Chang et al., Integrating Cultural Humility, 271.

13. Elmer, *Cross-cultural Servanthood*, 32.

position with the other person.[14] This self-examination is especially critical when working with those of minority cultures. It is too easy for a person from the dominant culture to take over and ignore the needs of the one from the minority, even though one might have good intentions overall. Those are not enough.

After much study and review of varying ideas surrounding the concept of cultural humility, John and Eloise believe the key concepts of cultural humility are formulated around the following core themes:

1. Building relationships: the key foundational component;

2. Intentional listening: gathering information, listening to the needs of people;

3. Setting aside predetermined biases and assumptions and critically examining them in light of new information and knowledge;

4. Collaboration and co-learning; learning with and from one another.

Key Concept 1:
Cultural Humility and Relationships

One of the core values of cultural humility is that of *relationship building*. Any successful work or ministry must first be built on this important value. Without honest and trusted relationships, it is difficult to begin, much less carry out or sustain effective programs or ministry. Too often the tendency is to rush through any initial stages of a program because we have our own preconceived agenda or timeline we need to meet. We want to be efficient in our work and make noticeable progress, which is the goal of Western-based cultures who are used to completing projects in a timely manner so that we feel we have accomplished something.[15] In developing-world cultures such as Kenya, the cultural practices place the person and the relationship first before any process or agenda. Intentional relationship building must never be trumped by any plans or timelines we may have made beforehand. The individual person or group needs to be the priority and should supersede any planned agenda.

Relationship building must be undertaken *with* the other—spending intentional time with the people, getting to know them and their families,

14. Chang et al., Integrating Cultural Humility, 269–278.

15. Lingenfelter and Mayers, *Ministering cross-culturally*, 41.

learning the culture, walking their paths and roads, and staying where they stay if at all possible. In the book *White Man Walking*, businessman Ward Brehm writes about his experiences in the Pokot region of Kenya and his friend Lodinyo.[16] When Lodinyo came to visit Ward in the U.S., Ward's wife mentioned how wonderful it was to have him in their home since Ward had been to Lodinyo's community many times. However, Lodinyo disagreed with the definition of Ward's visits. Lodinyo told Ward, when you come you are only with your people and stay in a separate house. Ward was shocked by this response but realized Lodinyo was correct. Ward had never walked Lodinyo's road in such a way as to authentically get to know him.

In most cultures, relationship building often begins with the *breaking of bread* together. Tea times and meals are especially important in the Kenyan culture, where the daily tea and meals bring people together and create special bonds that are sometimes difficult for Westerners to understand. This concept of breaking bread together is one that is highlighted many times in Scripture as Jesus met with his disciples and others over food in their homes. Eating together and hospitality in this way is also a spiritual experience and contributes significantly to the relationship-building endeavor.

Early on in Eloise and John's working relationship, Eloise was invited to stay with John and his wife, Rose, in their home within John's family compound located in the village of Kivagala. For Eloise, it was an honor to be invited not just for tea or a meal, but to stay overnight with this family. She was able to spend several nights there with the family engaging in fellowship before returning to the U.S. As John was driving Eloise to the airport the morning she was to leave, he said to her, "You have now stayed in my home." Then he was silent. Eloise was a little puzzled at his comment, but then replied, "Yes, I have stayed in your home." John continued the conversation by stating, "I have stayed in the homes of Americans, and now you have stayed in my home." At that point Eloise began to realize the significance of the conversation. John was seeking a form of approval for himself and his wife, knowing that Eloise, as an American, had much more materially than they did. Eloise finally found the right words and responded to John, saying, "John, it was such a blessing to stay in your home. I had all of my needs met. I was loved, cared for, given food to eat, a bed to sleep in, and shared wonderful hospitality." That answer satisfied John and the conversation moved on to other things. As Eloise and John have since

16. Brehm, *White Man Walking*, 14–16.

reflected on that initial overnight stay at the Muhanji homestead, they both believe that particular example was a significant turning point for their professional relationship and ministry in the total acceptance of the other regardless of economic status or background.

In another example related to hospitality, Eloise's dear Kenyan friend Violet shared a personal story with Eloise about the importance of sharing meals together and respect for culture. Violet is a successful educator in Kenya, and at the time of this writing is the principal of a large girls' boarding school in western Kenya. Violet often receives many guests at her school, including guests from other countries. As one example, educators from a Western-based country paid Violet and her school a visit just a few days before Eloise came. Violet's staff had prepared a lovely spread of food of varying sorts, typical of Kenyan fare. However, these visitors refused her food, saying they had brought their own. Violet later discovered their food consisted of snacks with granola bars and dried fruits. Violet was deeply hurt and offended that these visitors refused her food. By refusing Violet's food, they had also refused her hospitality, which was a greater personal and cultural insult. As Violet shared this story, Eloise was visiting with her doctoral student Andrea Nelson. Violet told the both of them after lunch the first day, "I was watching to see if you would eat my food." Eloise and Andrea replied, "Of course we would eat your food! You prepared it for us and it was most delicious!" This interaction immediately deepened the friendship and relationships between Eloise, Violet, and Andrea.

Eloise and Andrea learned another valuable lesson about the importance of forging strong relationships while at Violet's school. Andrea had traveled to Kenya in order to gather her dissertation data through interviews of Quaker secondary school principals. Isaac, one principal Eloise knew from his participation with previous curriculum projects, had been invited as one of Andrea's participants. Isaac shared the following story with Eloise and Andrea. When he was invited to the interview, he became quite nervous. He told Eloise and Andrea that in Kenya when one is summoned to an interview, that person must prepare in advance. Isaac called Violet, the organizer for the interviews, and asked how to prepare since he wanted to be sure he had prepared adequately. Violet told him, "Just come." But Isaac relayed to the women he felt he had to prepare something. He could not arrive at such an interview unprepared—it would be totally unprofessional according to his standards. Isaac was quite anxious as the day arrived and he reported to Violet's school for the interview. When Isaac entered the room where Andrea was interviewing the participants, he saw Eloise, walked over to where she was sitting, and they quickly exchanged greetings before the interview started. After the interview was over, Isaac recapped this entire story and concluded by stating to Eloise, "When I saw you when I came in, all my anxieties disappeared because I knew you!" Eloise was taken by surprise at his comment, but it has since become an important lesson to remember about the significance of forging good strong relationships with others!

Eloise experienced another example of the value of strong relationships during one of her visits to Muliro Village. As she was engaged in conversation with one of the teachers from Musembe Primary School, the teacher asked Eloise how much it cost for a plane ticket to Kenya. When Eloise told her the amount, the teacher was quite taken back, especially since it was more than half of her yearly salary. Then the teacher started to wonder out loud what could be done if Eloise just sent the money. After a few sentences of exploring various ideas, the teacher suddenly stopped and said to Eloise, "Oh no, it is not the money, it is not about the money. We need you here. It is important for you to be here with us." Her last statement revealed to Eloise the importance of the relationship building that had taken place within the village. Just sending money to the region could not replace the relationships and learning from each other that had been taking place for several years.

Relationship building through the lens of *cultural humility* in any setting global or locally has several key components. The first is: We are all made in the image of God and each person has value. Taking the time to get to know someone acknowledges their unique value as a human being in God's kingdom who can contribute even in a small way to any program or initiative. We must never take that for granted. This is especially true when working within another culture. Eloise's institution, George Fox University, has a two-word phrase that drives the philosophy of relationships across the campus: *Be Known.* Simple, yet profound. During Eloise's trips to Kenya, she has experienced many times the power of *Be Known.* The story of Emily is one such example.

Eloise and one of her colleagues, Scot Headley, had been invited to give an educational lecture during a professional development workshop session for principals and leaders from the Quaker secondary schools. Eloise recognized some of the participants from previous workshops where a team of George Fox faculty and Kenyan school leaders developed and wrote the *Curriculum for Peace and Conflict Management* for the Quaker secondary schools. As Eloise was greeting the participants of this particular workshop, she shook the hand of one female teacher and said to her, "Emily, it is good to see you again!" When Eloise finished her greeting, Emily froze in place with a look of astonishment on her face. Tears began to stream down her face as she said, "You remembered my name, you remembered my name!" Eloise replied, "Of course I did! I worked with you on the peace curriculum project!" Eloise and Emily then shared a number of conversations and interactions throughout the remainder of the workshop. Remembering someone's name seems very basic, but it is of the utmost importance in relationship building, as it helps people to know that they have value and matter. These encounters are critical reminders for all of our work with people of any culture, whether in the U.S. or abroad. Acknowledging people first, their worth, and building relationships with them must be the primary objective of any work or initiative we undertake within a local context or in global service.

Another key component of relationship building includes the principle: *Your insights matter and are valued.* Early on in Eloise's work with John and others in Kenya, she quickly realized she needed to rely on the Kenyans she and her colleagues were working with, especially John. He was the liaison for his organization, Friends United Meeting, and the George Fox University team. While Eloise and her colleagues had expertise in many areas related to educational initiatives, they did not have the cultural understanding, knowledge, or insights that could move any of their projects to completion. As the George Fox team and Kenyan school leaders continued with their very first project, the development of the *Curriculum for Peace and Conflict Management*, the expertise of John and the Kenyan school leaders was vital to the successful completion and implementation of the peace curriculum. One of Eloise's younger Kenyan friends, Kevin, commented to her during one of her visits regarding the principals and teachers, "These people are capable and smart, they just lack the resources and opportunities you have had." This young man made a keen observation that continues to resonate through John and Eloise's work. Within the attitude of cultural humility, the George Fox team willingly and wholeheartedly learned to listen to the Kenyans' voices, perspectives, and experience. But more importantly, the George Fox team needed to learn *from* the Kenyans. Their collective voice and knowledge was critical in providing the appropriate and culturally relevant materials for the peace curriculum project and others to follow.

The final key component of relationship building can be summarized as: *Respect the culture*. Part of relationship building centers on respecting the culture of those with whom we are working. Every culture has their own traditions, processes, language, and customs which are deeply rooted into daily life. Many of these customs are difficult for Westerners to notice and understand at the surface level, especially within a short timeframe. Therefore, it is imperative that we acknowledge we do not fully know that culture with all of its nuances and unspoken rules and procedures. We must continue to view ourselves as the guest in that culture and rely on the native representatives to guide our ongoing interactions and learning.

There are many specific examples of cultural protocols from every country, but in this book we will speak to respecting Kenyan cultural norms. One example of cultural protocols in Kenya involves the opening session of meetings. In Kenya, meetings often begin with a historical overview of the issue, or what has occurred in the past that has led to the present context. At times, this process could seem redundant or unnecessary to those from other cultures. However, the value of this process is that everyone at the meeting has the framework for the background and the meeting begins with all participants on the same page.

Seating arrangements are another interesting cultural dynamic. The placement of people in a carefully chosen order indicates their rank or status at that particular meeting. A head table in a meeting is very common, with the main leaders seated in the front. Even seating placement in vehicles has importance. When working and staying on Mt. Elgon, Eloise's students have found it interesting that when one of their hosts, Harry, arrived on site to greet them, the seating arrangements in the vehicles changed. Eloise was directed to ride with Harry in the lead car, and the others followed behind in the other vehicle. Since Harry was host of the guests, and chairman of board for Kaptama hospital, the cultural protocols were carefully adhered to according to the customs of that region.

Eloise related an interesting experience of seating arrangements at one of the Yearly Meeting sessions, the annual denominational conference gathering for the Quakers in Kenya. She and John arrived after the meeting had started and tried to slip in the side door of the church without causing too much "commotion," as John referred to it. That strategy completely failed. John was of course immediately recognized because of his role as director of the African Ministries Office (AMO). Therefore, the cultural protocol meant that he was to be seated on the stage. Eloise, as a White visitor, was obviously the lone minority in attendance, but her status as visitor also meant she was to be seated on the stage. While the meeting proceeded, several people quickly shuffled the seating arrangements on the stage and moved people around so John and Eloise could be seated on the stage in primary positions. In addition, the moving of chairs continued so John and Eloise could have the soft padded chairs as well, further indicating their status for that meeting.

Another interesting cultural insight especially from church meetings is that a prayer does not automatically mean a meeting has ended. A number of times Eloise has stood up after a concluding prayer thinking the meeting was over, and John has had to motion to her to sit back down because the meeting still had not been properly concluded. As Eloise notes, she is still learning this lesson and tries to wait for John's cue that a meeting has actually concluded before she makes any inappropriate movement to leave.

One cultural protocol contributed to Eloise missing her in-country flight to Nairobi at the end of one her visits. John had wanted to stop at one of the Yearly Meeting sessions to greet the people and encourage them in their work. As Eloise wrote in her journal, she knew that the timing to get to the airport and make her flight would be tight as soon as she and John had arrived at the church where the meeting was taking place. Tea time was already more than an hour late, and a number of events were still scheduled to take place before the main sermon started. Eloise already knew from previous visits that those events would most likely not be rescheduled. The sermon was lengthy but Eloise held out hope she could still make her flight. Right at the conclusion of the sermon, a politician entered the meeting, and all attention turned to him. Now the meeting was suddenly held hostage by this arrogant politician, but due to the cultural norms, John could not just get up and leave. He had to officially be released by the clerk (chairperson) of the meeting. The politician was given the floor to greet the people, and the church meeting soon turned into a political venue for the politician. The situation was frustrating for Eloise since she had a flight to the U.S. to catch out of Nairobi later that evening. Once John was finally released to leave the meeting, he rushed Eloise to the airport. As they got to the airport, Eloise's flight had just taken off. In situations where cultural protocols seem to take forever or are forgotten, John has stated several times, "Even my own culture sometimes drives me crazy!"

One example relating to respecting cultural processes occurred when Eloise was traveling with a group of educators from another country. These educators were visiting various schools in Kenya in order to gain a comprehensive view of the Kenyan educational system. John and his office staff had scheduled at least two and sometimes three school visits each day, which meant for long days and sometimes a rushed visit at each school. One day while visiting a school in the early afternoon, one of the other educators abruptly stood up and announced it was time to leave and move on to the next school. The Kenyan hosts were taken off guard since their processes and procedures had been usurped by a foreigner. The situation became quite uncomfortable and the Kenyans tried to wrap up the visit according to their protocols and customs while trying to respect the sudden demands of this foreigner. The lesson in this experience was that John and his team knew very well what the schedule and timeline was, but culturally the visit was not over until the cultural protocols had been completed. This educator had been completely out of line with her demands and it caused tension with the Kenyan hosts at that school. Further, the attention was then focused on her instead of the purpose for the visit to the school. Processes in any culture are important and really do matter.

Relationship building is intentional and takes time. It is important to learn people's names (even pronouncing the names correctly), some of the culture, and even basic words in the language. This also means we must listen to people, treat them as equals, eat with them, pray with them, stay where they are staying, fellowship with them, learn with them, walk the road with them, learn to love them as Jesus loves them, and find ways to connect with them in meaningful and authentic ways. Only after we are intentionally forming ongoing and trustworthy relationships should we consider enter into meaningful work and ministry together.

Key Concept 2:
Cultural Humility and Intentional Listening

The second tenet of cultural humility is *careful and intentional listening*. This tenet aligns with the scripture from James 1:19, which admonishes us to be "quick to listen" and "slow to speak." Establishing honest and trustworthy relationships is foundational to our interactions and work with individuals and groups both locally and globally. But in order to develop these types of relationships at a deeper level, we must actively practice being *quick to listen and slow to speak*. In Duane Elmer's book *Cross-Cultural Servanthood: Serving the World in Christlike Humility*, he refers to the work of William Stringfellow, who believes that true listening is not a common occurrence among people.[17] If we truly reflect on that statement, there is much truth to it. Our human tendencies are more likely to be *quick to speak* and *slow to listen*, while we are already formulating a response. As we consider the biblical principle of being *quick to listen and slow to speak*, each of us should try a little experiment. Intentionally observe yourself and others in meetings and conversations. Ask yourself the following questions:

1. How often do I anticipate what others are going to say?

2. How often do I try to finish the sentences or thoughts of others without allowing them to completely finish?

3. How often am I formulating responses as another person is talking?

4. Am I distracted when in conversation with someone else?

There are many positive reasons for practicing the principles of being *quick to listen and slow to speak*, but here are just a few. We first become a learner as we listen with the motivation of learning instead of focusing on the reply or response. The posture of the learner takes on the cloak and attitude of humility, *sitting at the feet* of someone else to learn from them. Duane Elmer also notes that people often share at a deeper level when they know the other person is really listening to them. He also believes that as we are truly listening to others, they "have access to our mind and heart."[18] After we have intentionally taken the time to listen, clarifying questions can help deepen our understanding of the other person's views, ideas, and ultimately their needs.

Intentional listening also allows us to learn from multiple perspectives. How often is our view of something limited or narrow because we have not considered a different perspective? How often have we dismissed the view of another because their perspective seems different or even *foreign* to us? Through intentional listening we demonstrate respect and honor to the other person. Intentional listening means that we have to slow down. It means not interrupting or anticipating how we are going to respond, or

17. Elmer, *Cross-cultural Servanthood*, 121.

18. Ibid., 122.

completing someone else's thoughts. Practicing effective listening skills is yet another critical step in building strong and trusted relationships in all areas of our lives.

It is helpful to acknowledge and remember that when working with those from other cultures, we generally are limited in our knowledge of the culture and their common practices. We often do not have all of the pertinent information we need to make informed suggestions or to give advice. In fact, most of the time we have no business giving any kind of advice until we have formed trustworthy relationships and have been asked for our advice or opinion. Eloise has traveled in Kenya with a variety of people from the U.S. and elsewhere and has gathered many examples of well-meaning but inappropriate *advice giving*. Many times she has heard some fellow travelers with good intentions offer advice to John without him asking for it. Typically, the advice is framed within the limited perspective of the person giving it, and without enough background information to make the advice even worthy to be considered. John always graciously and patiently responds to the unsolicited advice in such a way that the person soon learns about the issues with the corresponding challenges. The better approach for anyone in an unfamiliar culture or situation would be to utilize good questioning strategies in order to gain a comprehensive view of the issue as best as possible. Those questions can include examples such as:

- Tell me how you do . . . ?
- What experiences have you had with . . . ?
- In our country we do something like. . . . Would that even work here?
- What are your challenges with this issue?
- What kinds of solutions have you or others tried? How has that approach worked?

Intentional listening must take priority in order for us to learn and gather as much information as possible. Only then can we begin to ask informed questions to assist with our learning about the culture, and resist providing unsolicited advice. This tendency is especially difficult for those from Western-based cultures who may have superior attitudes toward other cultures, believing their way is the only way to accomplish the task or objective. Cultural humility with the posture of intentional listening can help provide us a different perspective that takes the focus off of ourselves and places it on others. Only then we can become a true learner and listener.

Key Concept 3:
Cultural Humility and Addressing Biases and Assumptions

Another very critical component of cultural humility is *checking our own biases and assumptions*. This can be a very difficult topic to engage with, but we need to first begin with ourselves and our own backgrounds. As Eloise notes, her biases and assumptions were first shaped as she was growing up within her family and community. Eloise was raised in a small town in northern Minnesota, which was very White and very non-diverse. She notes that she did not even know a person of color until an African American young man came to her high school to play football with the varsity football team. She did not even experience any other kind of ethnic food until she was in college. In a nutshell, Eloise just was not exposed to anything else other than traditional Midwest living in a very small bubble. Her parents were middle class and worked hard, the family was heavily involved in church activities, and Eloise's life was surrounded with people the same as her. She recounts that some of her relatives often talked negatively about different people groups, demonstrating the relatives' biases. Eloise never liked to hear them talk that way and it made her feel uncomfortable, but it was the language she heard and she did not know how to respond at that point in her life. Now many years later after much travel and developing friendships with people from many backgrounds, Eloise is able to view each person as created in God's image, and advocate for their uniqueness within the body of Christ as bearing the image of God himself.

On the other side of the world, John grew up in a small village in western Kenya as the last child in a family of seven. In John's adolescence years, John's father was a traveling minister who relied on the donations of others for his income and to support his family. John notes that as he entered high school, he did not even have the funds to completely pay for his schooling. Yet, he trusted his father when he told John that the rest of the money would come. The money eventually did come and John was able to remain in school on a full government-sponsored scholarship until he finished high school. John spent his growing up years in that small community, remaining there and not venturing beyond those boundaries until he went to college. It was after his college years and he accepted a job at the Central Bank of Kenya that his eyes were opened to other ways of life and thinking. During those years at the bank John interacted with people who were different than he was, which helped to shape his perspectives as an adult and prepare him for his future ministry.

Even though Eloise and John had vastly different life experiences in their growing and formative years, they continually work to overcome their own ingrained biases and assumptions in order to work with each other and others around the world. Each person carries certain biases which are formed through each individual personal experience. Those biases, left unchecked, can become a barrier in how one engages with those who are different than we are. It is too easy to generalize the characteristics of a group of people without realizing that there are many differences within those groups. Those generalizations can then influence the ways in which we engage with those people, for the positive or the negative. No matter one's background, complete with her or his own unique biases and assumptions, God takes each person as they are, where they are, and expands the boundaries of their ways of thinking and perspectives in order for them to become the person he wants them to be, in order to build relationships and better engage with others.

We all probably have many stories about incorrect assumptions or biases we have had toward others, or that others have had toward us. In Duane Elmer's book, he writes about a study that took place in America. The researchers wanted to know how fast Americans would make judgments about certain people or people groups when first meeting them. In how many seconds do you think it takes until we make those kinds of initial judgments? Answer: 2.4—4.6 seconds. Amazing. And, those judgments are usually based on "surface characteristics," which are very narrow in scope. That study should give us pause to think. The same study also showed that, given opportunity, we could change our mind about our initial judgment.[19] However, most of our initial judgments are not accurate and we quickly form unfounded conclusions. Eloise had an experience recently when on a hiring committee for an outside organization. Eloise relayed some of her leadership experiences from her university work that could be helpful in the hiring process. Another committee member revealed her surprise and confusion as she said to Eloise, "I had no idea you were involved with leadership. I always assumed you just worked with music teachers." This other member's comment was interesting on two different accounts. First, she had made an assumption about what kind of work Eloise did based on some of her hobbies and talents. Secondly, the committee member had

19. Ibid., 48.

never asked Eloise what her role was at the university even though both had known each other for quite a while. The information was based on incorrect assumptions alone.

As a part of the topic of examining biases, assumptions, and stereotypes, Eloise came across a TED Talk that helps to shed further light on this topic. Chimamanda Ngozi Adichie, a Nigerian author, shares her personal experiences of inaccurate assumptions in "The Danger of a Single Story." She notes how her college roommates in the States made many assumptions about her life in Nigeria. They asked to hear her songs on her iPod thinking it would be African music, but were disappointed when she had American pop music on her playlists. Some of her professors did not believe she could write the quality of stories she did knowing she came from Africa. Adichie's story is a reminder of how initial impressions and assumptions can be inaccurate and indeed become a single story without gathering more information.[20]

Eloise experienced an example of assumptions when she was visiting another non-governmental organization (NGO) in Kenya. The office director of this NGO, Florence (name changed), had invited Eloise to have tea with one of the local women leaders, Lillian, in her home. As Eloise, Florence, and another worker were walking down the dusty road, Florence began to ask Eloise many questions about her experiences in Kenya. Florence was explaining that Lillian belonged to a different ethnic group and Florence wanted to be sure that Eloise was comfortable going into Lillian's home for tea. Eloise responded it was no problem because she had met many different Kenyans before and she was eager to have tea with this woman. Florence then proceeded to ask Eloise about the food she ate while in Kenya. Eloise responded that she ate the local food whenever it was offered to her: ugali, sukuma wiki, other kinds of green vegetables, cassava, sweet potatoes, cabbage, and whatever was in season. Florence was amazed that Eloise had eaten so many different varieties of foods and even liked them. Florence continued her questioning and asked Eloise where she generally stayed while in the country. Eloise replied that as much as possible she stays in the homes of her Kenyan friends in order to spend time with them and learn from them. Finally, Florence blurted out in amazement, "You actually stay in the homes of Kenyans?!" Eloise affirmed that she had just come from John and Rose's home, where she had been for almost a week. Florence then shook her head as she said, "You certainly are not like any American

---

20. Adichie, *The Danger of a Single Story*, TEDGlobal, 2009.

I have ever met!" Eloise was rather taken back by this statement and took time to process Florence's words. While Eloise viewed the statement as a compliment, she was also very concerned about the impressions that other Americans had been leaving on Florence and other Kenyans. In this case, Florence had made certain assumptions about Eloise based on previous experiences with Americans, but Eloise did not match those assumptions.

Eloise relates another story about checking one's own filter of biases and assumptions that occurred with one of her graduate students, Gloria (name changed), during a visit to Kenya. As Gloria was visiting with a school principal about the daily schedule, she learned that each subject had only thirty minutes a day for instruction. Gloria believed this was not nearly enough time for teachers and students to learn the content, and she began to brainstorm how the school could add more teaching time. She came up with the idea that if the school took out the daily tea time, there would be more instructional time in the schedule and the students could learn more. However, Gloria stated later, after she had a revelation about her original thinking, "But tea time is important to their culture, and it was an ah-ha moment that I should not take away something I am finding very beautiful about their culture and replace it with things." This example demonstrates how easy it can be to offer a solution without understanding the cultural contexts involved.

John recounts his own missteps in his ministry with an issue regarding assumptions and biases. Early in his ministry work with Friends United Meeting, John traveled to Tanzania for the purposes of visiting the Quaker work in that country. This particular trip took him to one of the churches that was in a very humble community. As John looked around and saw the dilapidated building with the crumbling ceiling and walls, he began to scold the people for not caring about the condition of the building and ignoring their duty to maintain the facility. Not long after this incident, John discovered this was a very small congregation with very few resources. The people had been using their meager resources to minister to the neighboring community instead of using their funds for the building. After John learned additional details of this congregation, John was immediately ashamed of his attitude and the way he made incorrect assumptions about this church group. John also later discovered that his scolding deeply affected the church people and they eventually lost their motivation and desire to continue their ministry and the church almost closed. John admits and deeply regrets he had spoken from the lens of a *single story*.

This unfortunate example was a strong lesson for John about not making assumptions about people or their conditions, but instead to uplift and encourage the people at whatever point they are in their ministry.

God has uniquely created all of us and values diversity and the unique individuals we all are. Building relationships and being quick to listen and slow to speak both play a part in breaking down barriers of biases and assumptions, which then allows us to see people as God sees them. As we enter into various situations, whether in our culture or that of another, we bring our own filter or biases into that experience. Our own way of thinking and seeing things is impacted by our family structure, upbringing, prior experiences, education, and many more factors. Working with others requires that we recognize our own biases first and then make concerted attempts to view situations from multiple perspectives in order to understand the situation as best as possible. We all have limitations with regard to understanding the culture of another. As we enter into collaboration work with others either locally or globally, checking our own biases and assumptions is a starting point for positive and healthy interactions. Lingenfelter and Mayers note that "knowing one's cultural bias is essential to effective ministry."[21]

Key Concept 4:
Cultural Humility with Collaboration
and Co-Learning Strategies

The final tenet of the *cultural humility* framework is that of *collaboration*. True collaboration effectively combines the components of *relationship building, being quick to listen and slow to speak, and challenging our biases and assumptions*. These components together promote a co-learning mode of working with others. A collaborative or co-learning approach takes into consideration the needs, opinions, ideas, background, culture, and experiences of the other person or groups. Further, authentic collaboration builds on common relationships where we can view collaboration as a sacrament toward the other. The attitude of sacrament means we cast aside our pride and begin the collaboration on an equal plane with others. This concept of sacrament in our work is also an attitude of living in an honest relationship with others. For example, when the principles of collaboration are applied

21. Lingenfelter and Mayers, *Ministering Cross-culturally*, 12.

holistically in a medical context, the patient has direct input and feedback regarding his or her own care, thus removing the physician from the all-powerful and all-knowing role, and creating a collaborative approach to health care with the patient.[22] Both the patient and physician then work together to come up with an appropriate treatment plan. In education, there would also be many applications of a collaborative model when working with families, planning teams, data teams, administrative teams, professional learning communities, and parent groups in order to build trusted relationships.[23] The same principles of collaboration apply in any kind of ministry work as well.

The opposite of a collaborative approach would be a coercion model, which forces a preconceived agenda and ultimately takes away the input and ideas of those with whom we are working. Reaching a true mode of *collaboration* means that each of us also must recognize our own tendencies to assert our own position, views, and ideas over those of others. As previously stated, this tendency to assert one's agenda is common for those from Western or dominant cultures who may believe that their culture is superior to the one with whom they are working. Cultural humility, paired with collaboration, weaves together the ideas and perspectives of all parties involved without any one side dominating or taking control of the process, thus honoring the diversity of the other.

In the resource information from a simple Kenyan trainers' manual, the authors share a framework for how best to engage with others at various levels leading to a collaborative model. The participatory continuum, starting with "co-option" and moving toward "cooperation," illustrates that the ultimate goal of one's collaborative work should be projects that utilize the skills and abilities of the target community, as opposed to reducing those community members to a passive role, such as found in the "co-option" level.[24] The following table, adapted from de Negri et al., shows the interaction levels.[25]

---

22. Tervalon and Murray-Garcia, Cultural Humility Versus Cultural Competence, 121.

23. Ross, Notes from the Field, 316.

24. de Negri, *Empowering Communities*, session 2, 8.

25. Ibid., session 2, 8.

Type of Participation	Involvement of Local People	Relationship to Local People
Co-option	Representatives have no real power.	On
Compliance	Outsiders decide and direct the process.	For
Consultation	Locals are asked; outsiders analyze and decide actions.	For/with
Cooperation	Locals work with outsiders; responsibilities remain with outsiders.	With
Co-learning	Local people and outsiders share knowledge; outsiders facilitate.	With/by
Collective Action	Local people set own agenda without outsiders.	By

The Participatory Continuum

While there are times when the co-option approach of *doing on* or *for* might be appropriate, such as in crisis response situations, it would never be acceptable as a long-term approach. Cross-cultural work and interactions must lead toward the goal of collective action, which ultimately leaves the power with the other culture. Richard Slimbach notes from his work on global learning:

> As outsiders, we have the opportunity to bridge the global gap by relying on and learning from the expertise, strengths, and collective wisdom of the community. . . . We work at the behest of local groups on local projects led by local people addressing local issues with local resources.[26]

This is the model of cultural humility in practice.

John relates an example of a collaboration effort in Kenya that involved a container of medical supplies. During one of John's visits to the States, he worked with a group of people to identify specific medical supplies needed for one of the Quaker medical facilities in Kenya. John accompanied the representatives of this particular group to a medical supply store and together they carefully selected the supplies the medical facility in Kenya had identified as the top priorities. When John returned to Kenya, he believed that everything was in order and he would be receiving the container in Kenya within a few months. However, things did not go as planned. Since this was also a time period when many supplies were also being sent to Haiti for

26. Slimbach, *Becoming World Wise*, 34–35.

relief efforts, the supplies designated for John's container were redirected to another container for Haiti. The group in the States making the decisions for the medical supplies decided to fill the container with different supplies. They believed that since the container was going to Africa anyway, these supplies could also be used there as well.

As the container was headed to Kenya, several issues were discovered while it was in route to the port of entry. First, since the original supplies had suddenly been shifted to a different container, the inventory for the current supplies in the container was not correct, thus creating errors with the shipping manifest. The incorrect manifest produced many issues as the container entered the port and all of the documentation was not in order. The container sat in port in Kenya for many weeks incurring mounting storage fees as the issues were sorted out so that the container could be released. Finally, the container was released, but only after John's organization paid over $6,000 in fees and interest. Once the container reached its final destination, the supplies that had been sent were not the items desperately needed for this medical facility and the surrounding community.

The container example gives us many lessons in the area of collaboration and co-learning. First, John knew the needs of the medical facility and was acting on its behalf to obtain the necessary supplies. The supplies were carefully selected and he believed those would be in the container when it arrived in Kenya. The group John was working with in the States decided to redirect the supplies without having any understanding of the process of true collaboration and understanding the needs of that particular facility. The group made an incorrect assumption that just because the supplies were going to Africa, they could be used. Finally, because of the incorrect manifest, John's organization had to pay a large sum of money for unnecessary supplies. That money could have been prioritized for other ministry efforts, but instead went to pay for someone else's incorrect assumptions about the needs of the people they thought they were helping.

In another example of the importance of the collaborative process in local and global efforts, John tells a story of how collaboration was ignored as a group in the States made assumptions about what was needed at different medical facility. This example also involved a container. In this case, several members of this group had been to Kenya a number of times assisting in this other medical facility. The group discovered that this facility needed a number of supplies in order to further their work with the community. When the members of this group returned to the States, they organized for a container in order to send the necessary medical supplies. As the group was preparing the container, they suddenly thought of other things they could also include in the container, thus using the space and sending a full container. When the container arrived in the Kenyan port, the medical facility discovered that the extra supplies which had been added were large amounts of clothing. The group from the States had made an assumption that the people in Kenya could use the clothes, not thinking that Kenyans can easily purchase clothes in their own country. The medical supplies were not subject to taxes, but the clothes were taxable items. The medical facility ended up having to pay a large amount of tax for the clothes in order to get the medical supplies. Further, the hospital incurred a large debt and for several months they could not even pay their employees.

The lesson for this example relates directly back to assumptions. The collaboration attempts were initially in place, but when the group in the States made additional assumptions without first consulting their Kenyan partners, the collaborative effort broke down as this group shifted to acting on what they perceived to be the needs of the Kenyans. The clinic staff in Kenya become demoralized as they suffered personal loss as a result of the incorrect assumptions of this American group. In this case, helping did hurt.

Conclusion

While the concept and framework of cultural humility can provide guidance to any cross-cultural initiative, whether local or global, it is in no way a set model for how one should engage in cross-cultural work. John and Eloise believe that using these four main tenets of cultural humility can provide critical guidance to one's work, while still allowing for nimbleness and fluidity to meet the needs of any cross-cultural initiative.

The following chapters further explain the collaborative work Eloise and John have been involved with in Kenya, utilizing the lessons and principles of cultural humility.

2

Developing the Secondary Peace Curriculum for the Quaker Schools in Kenya

JOHN AND ELOISE'S CROSS-CULTURAL collaborative work began in 2009 with the development of the *Curriculum for Peace and Conflict Management*. This curriculum was created out of nothing from the ground up, bringing together a team of educators from George Fox University and educational leaders from the Quaker secondary schools in Kenya working side by side to accomplish the task. The peace curriculum was the first collaborative project that connected George Fox University colleagues with Quaker education colleagues from Kenya. Additionally, this first collaborative project set the stage for additional educational work in Kenya, and demonstrates how all of the components of *cultural humility* were infused into this first project.

In 2007–2008, Kenya experienced post-election violence which riveted through the entire nation. More than one thousand people were killed and thousands displaced from their homes. The post-election violence revealed the urgency and need to teach peace and conflict-resolution skills, beginning first with students in the nation's schools, since the main perpetrators of the violence were school-age young people and community idlers. The Quaker church, known as promoters of peace and also sponsors of many schools, was especially concerned about the violence since many students from the Quaker schools participated in the destruction within the communities.

Prior to the violence, a team of educators from the Quaker secondary schools in Kenya had been meeting with John to fervently discuss how to integrate peace concepts into the curriculum of the Quaker schools. The violence demonstrated the need for such a curriculum and this group of leaders desired to move forward with an initiative to create a peace curriculum that was tailored specifically to Kenyan culture and schools. At that point in time, nothing like it existed that would meet their unique needs as a nation.

Just a few months after the violence, John sent an email to several other institutions in the U.S. with the hopes of collaborating with one of them on the proposed peace curriculum project. When those attempts for collaboration fell through, John remembered an acquaintance at George Fox University and sent him an email. In this introductory email, John inquired about the possibility of George Fox University collaborating with the Kenyan Quaker secondary school leadership team to help develop a curriculum for peace and conflict management. Once John's request had been received, a select team from the School of Education gathered together to study the feasibility of engaging in such a collaborative effort. This initial team represented professors from the School of Education who had experience in curriculum design and writing, international and other cross-cultural experience, professional development, secondary education, and peace and conflict work.

After several meetings of the George Fox planning team, which included prayerful discussions and discernment, the team agreed they had clarity to move forward and assist with the peace curriculum project. The George Fox team had no idea what to expect, nor could they anticipate any possible or potential final outcomes, but they ultimately agreed to take a step of faith and partner with the Quaker secondary school leadership.

As the George Fox team began the preliminary stages of the peace curriculum project, the primary goal of Eloise and her colleagues was that they would respect the collaborative process and carefully listen to the needs and desires of the Kenyan partners. That would be the first step in the relationship-building process. The George Fox team had limited knowledge of Kenyan culture, and virtually no background with the Kenyan secondary school structure. Even though these factors could have been considered a major disadvantage to the project, Eloise and her colleagues viewed it as an incredible opportunity for cross-cultural learning.

Once the George Fox team agreed to move forward with this project, the next step was to plan for on-site workshops in Kenya where both teams would gather to write the peace curriculum. The pre-workshop preparation had consisted of many emails back and forth between John and the George

Fox team, and a brief meeting of one of the George Fox team members with John and the Kenyan leadership a few months prior on site in Kenya. Eloise and her colleagues did their best to anticipate how the workshop sessions would be structured, and what kind of curriculum resources might be useful for the first workshop.

Upon arriving in Kenya for the first workshop, the George Fox team met the Kenyan participants of this project for the first time. This first curriculum workshop consisted of the team of four George Fox faculty members and ten Kenyans representing the secondary schools as either principals, retired educators, or church leaders. John oversaw the efforts for the Kenyan team in his role as director of the African Ministries Office for Friends United Meeting (FUM). Eloise wrote in her journal after the first evening that all participants seemed a bit nervous during their first meeting as together they embarked on this new journey into the unknown.

The opening session began with formal introductions and an outline for the sessions. Then Eloise and her colleagues began their work in earnest according to the plans they had made via email with the Kenyan team. When the first teaching block came to a conclusion in the mid-morning, the George Fox team huddled together for a quick debrief session. They all shared the feelings of dismay that the first teaching block had been a total failure, and in their opinion they felt the need to throw out all of the initial planning and start over. This was the first lesson in expectations and misguided assumptions about processes in the Kenyan culture. The George Fox team had particular assumptions about how the flow of a workshop should go according to timing and planning from a Western perspective, but they were unprepared for the *slowness* of their first workshop session all together with the teams from both sides. This was the first example of how the Kenyans viewed time. Every word and every part of the work would be carefully considered and scrutinized. The Kenyans did not appear to be in a hurry to complete the workshop sessions according to the timeline and plans of the Westerners. Further, as Eloise and her colleagues later learned, the event itself was more valued than what was accomplished during the workshop sessions.[1]

The George Fox team agreed to press on with the workshop after adapting and adjusting their plans by slowing down and taking more time to teach key concepts of curriculum development. They also took additional time for input from the participants, and patiently waited while the

---

1. Lingenfelter and Mayers, *Ministering Cross-culturally*, 41.

Kenyan team processed the information the GFU team presented. While the GFU team knew and understood the importance of this work, they also quickly recognized this project was going to take significantly more time than any of them had imagined. However, during the first day of the sessions, intentional relationship building was already taking place. Both teams were staying together in the same location, having all of their meals together, and more importantly, they were having many cups of tea together in fellowship. As John and Eloise later reflected, this first workshop and the intentional relationship building was the catalyst of other work in Kenya that would follow.

When the George Fox team began the planning of the workshop sessions, they made assumptions regarding how quickly the peace curriculum project could be completed. One of the GFU team members was an experienced writer and had published a number of curriculum and teaching pedagogy books, and he knew how long it usually took him to complete a project. In the early planning stages of the workshop, the GFU team set the original timeline to complete the peace curriculum project inside of a year if they moved quickly and with efficiency. The teams had planned for a final workshop three months after the first one in which all hoped they could finish the majority of the curriculum content. However, by the time the first workshop in Kenya ended after three days, the GFU team recognized the urgency for another workshop as soon as possible.

As the GFU team considered the importance of an additional workshop, they were also concerned about offending their Kenyan friends in requesting another workshop. These were all busy professionals and the GFU team worried about adding another set of meetings for this project. In order to continue the relationship-building process, the GFU team decided to involve the Kenyans in the discussions for a second workshop. One evening when the GFU team was debriefing the day's work, they invited one of the key advocates of this project, Alfred, to join their discussions. The GFU team openly shared their concerns about the slower progress of the project and that they were sensing the need for another workshop before the scheduled one in three months. The GFU team all listened carefully to Alfred's perspectives and rationale, and together all discerned that another workshop session was indeed necessary. Because of Alfred's leadership role, he agreed to handle the details and inform the rest of the Kenyan team of this added meeting. The next day when the idea was presented to the entire group, the Kenyans eagerly accepted the proposal and affirmed the urgency of this additional workshop. In fact, as all participants later discovered, they were most grateful for the commitment to ensuring that this project would move forward without delay. One of the key lessons in this particular situation was that Eloise and her colleagues involved Alfred as a key leader in the discussions, and asked for his input and advice. It was important for them to discern together and Alfred's support was key in the collaboration process. Further, it was at this point after only a few days together that the collaboration and co-learning had reached such a level that all recognized there were no longer two separate teams, but one development team.

From the onset of the peace curriculum project, the Kenyan leadership team desired to include active teaching strategies as a part of the curriculum's lessons and accompanying support materials. The Kenyans carefully explained that their system of education was deeply rooted in the antiquated colonial method of lectures, and teaching to the national test, thus creating a culture of passive learning for the students. The Kenyans believed that the teaching of the peace curriculum would need to move beyond the traditional lecture style, and incorporate teaching strategies in which the students actively participated in the content and were engaged in the lessons. Further, the Kenyans desired that the concepts of the peace curriculum would not be just head knowledge, but would become attitudinal and positively change the person's heart and actions.

In order to reach this goal, the development team needed to devise workshop sessions which would demonstrate student-centered (active) teaching strategies, as well as writing that style of teaching into the lesson plans. Since the GFU team already applied active teaching and learning pedagogy as a part of their own professional practice within their own university courses, they understood the requests from the Kenyan team. However, the GFU team also needed to be sure they were using and referring to the same educational language as their Kenyan partners.

Throughout the first workshop session, the group discussions not only included the content of the lessons, but the teaching strategies as well. The participants discussed every detail of the curriculum project, including layout of the written lesson plans, the terminology for the headings, and other details. The Kenyans wanted the written version of this peace curriculum project to match exactly what Kenyan teachers were used to seeing for the structure of their regular curriculum. Diverting from what was known would have cast a negative shadow on the project, and perhaps cause other teachers to ignore the curriculum if it did not follow a format they were accustomed to already using in their teaching.

Each session of the first workshop was geared to writing as many lessons as possible for the first draft of the peace curriculum. As the development team progressed in their time together, they began to share the leadership process of this first workshop, thus strengthening the relationship building. As stated previously, the entire process took longer than anticipated since every detail was discussed and sometimes debated. The Kenyans carefully scrutinized and critiqued each lesson so that they could improve on the overall development and avoid any passive learning lessons. During each session, the GFU team also invited their Kenyan partners to teach some parts of the draft lessons so that all had a visual representation of the desired outcome for the teaching. This process was valuable as the GFU team was able to watch their Kenyan colleagues teach and gauge their level of knowledge and expertise in active teaching strategies. On the last day of the first workshop session, Alfred volunteered to teach one of the newly written lessons. All participants were engaged in the process and impressed with his knowledge of active teaching pedagogy and his engagement with the content. He readily embraced the opportunity to teach in front of U.S. professors and gather feedback for his teaching skills.

At the close of the first workshop, the development team had written three complete lessons, with five more in draft stage. Even though Eloise and her colleagues experienced a bit of discouragement at the beginning of the first workshop, by the time it came to a conclusion the GFU team realized how much had been accomplished, not only with the development of the curriculum, but in what their team had learned about the Kenyan culture and schools, and the overall relationships they had begun to forge.

The second curriculum writing workshop took place on site in Kenya only two months after the first workshop. For the second workshop, Eloise brought along a different colleague, Suzanne Harrison, and together with the Kenya team began at the point the previous workshop had concluded. Most of the Kenyan leadership team remained the same, but with a few new faces to allow others to speak into the process. Since the relationship building and structure of the process had started in the first workshop, Eloise and Sue were able to transition a bit more smoothly into the work ahead of them. Their approach was to divide the participants into groups, write several lessons, then pass those lessons onto another group for editing and feedback. That way they would have many eyes and viewpoints on each lesson to examine for content, structure, and overall writing. Again, the content was driven by the Kenyans while Eloise and Sue provided the guidance for the overall curriculum structure and the word processing.

It was at this second workshop that Eloise and Sue wondered about visiting some of the schools. Both had a keen desire to learn more about their Kenyan partners with the intent to continue and deepen their newfound friendships. They also believed that school visits would inform their knowledge and understanding of the Kenyan schools, and provide key insights for the entire project. Eloise and Sue approached John with the school visit idea not knowing how he would respond. However, John eagerly agreed with the proposal and helped to map out a school visit to each of the eleven schools represented by teachers and principals in the workshop sessions. Once the second workshop concluded, John drove Eloise and Sue all over western Kenya in two and a half days to visit eleven different Quaker secondary schools of all types. This was a rewarding experience in itself, never to be forgotten.

The School Visits

Each school welcomed John, Eloise, and Sue with open arms and special activities to honor their visits. Students entertained with singing and dramas, and the three of them engaged in conversation with teachers, staff, and students. In the very first school they were treated to an observation of the first lesson from the peace curriculum. One of the younger teachers on the development team was assigned to teach the lesson to his class with the American professors and John in attendance. Both Eloise and Sue felt a bit of nervousness for the young man who was under such pressure with the important guests in attendance. However, this young teacher did an outstanding job and asked for feedback afterward in order to improve his teaching. The three visitors hoped this example could potentially be a model for how the curriculum would eventually be implemented and infused into the entire school curriculum. At the conclusion of the lesson, they were all served lunch, Kenyan style, with no utensils. This was a first for Eloise and Sue, but they proceeded to eat with their hands as their hosts did in order to demonstrate respect for this common cultural practice.

When John, Eloise, and Sue arrived at one of the boys' boarding schools later that first day, they were ushered in front of over nine hundred Kenyan young men who were standing at attention for the afternoon "parade" (assembly). After a few introductions, John instructed Eloise to "speak to the young men." As Eloise recalls, she experienced several moments of panic as she looked out at those nine hundred dark faces and wondered what on earth she, as a White female American professor, highly privileged, could say to these young men. She had a choice to rise to the occasion in her professional role, or decline and risk an opportunity to continue building relationships and trust with John and the other Kenyan leaders. Eloise chose to speak to the young men and was amazed at how God gave her the appropriate words to provide spiritual and academic encouragement. Sue was also invited to speak to the students, and John closed the session with powerful words of exhortations for these young men.

These school visits provided some of the necessary cultural background in helping Eloise and Sue better relate to the educational system and challenges of limited resources facing the Kenyan teachers and principals. Eloise and Sue were able to ask more informed questions, and not make assumptions about the schools. Kenyan schools are vastly different in their overall structure than American schools, thus the importance for the George Fox team to have this perspective to help change and challenge their cultural lens and assumptions. Even though the GFU team had tried to learn about the culture and schools prior to the first trip to Kenya via a Kenyan student who was attending George Fox, it was not even remotely enough. Visiting the schools on site was what impacted the peace curriculum work and brought it to the next level. The school visits also became an eye-opener for John, who since he had taken office at FUM several years prior had not really made formal visits to any of the schools. Even though he was a product of the Kenyan schools, these school visits were critical for the development of his ministry through Friends United Meeting.

Before Eloise and Sue left Kenya to travel home, the entire development team carefully laid plans for the next and hopefully final workshop. Once Eloise returned home, she carefully typed the lessons from the handwritten copies according to instructions from the Kenyans in order to prepare for the next workshop.

The third workshop session of the peace curriculum project occurred in August of 2009 and continued to build on the foundation established in the previous two sessions. Eloise came with yet another group of colleagues from George Fox, which included at that time her dean and department chair, along with one of the faculty members from the first workshop and her entire family. The Kenyan participants for this workshop were many of the same from the previous two workshops, but more teachers and principals had been invited to this session in order to garner additional input and support for this important project.

By the time the third workshop commenced, all of the original eleven schools represented in the development of the peace curriculum had piloted the first eight lessons of the curriculum within a six-week period. The teachers who had completed the pilot projects presented oral reports to the entire group about the teaching process and outcomes, then gave the participants opportunity to ask questions or provide feedback. One interesting development occurred during the oral presentations of the pilot lessons. One of the teachers who was a part of the development team and piloted the first eight lessons at her school had her students create posters that represented various concepts of conflict and resolution from the peace curriculum. She then shared these posters with the workshop participants as examples of how to engage students in the concepts in order to make them more meaningful for the students. These posters were so well received that the participants recommended they be incorporated into the printed version of the curriculum, thus providing concrete examples of possibilities with the teaching, as well as honoring the work of the Kenyan schools involved in the pilot teaching process.

As a part of this third workshop, Eloise and her colleagues provided printed copies of the curriculum which had been written and developed up to that point. The participants read and critiqued the information, discussed the various concepts, and provided additional insights to the work. Further, in the teaching sessions, the GFU team once again modeled active teaching strategies as a part of their instruction, and included selected Kenyans as collaborators in those teaching times. Once the workshop concluded, the development team, along with the remaining participants, agreed on a plan for how to move the curriculum to completion, hopefully within the following year. In just four short months a team of educators from the U.S. and leaders from the Quaker schools in Kenya had accomplished the almost impossible, and nearly completed a draft version of the *Curriculum for Peace and Conflict Management* for students in Form 1 (grade 9). The journey was not yet over, but all involved with the process were encouraged with the progress and collaboration that had already taken place.

All throughout the development of the peace curriculum, the Kenyan leadership team had been in constant contact with the Ministry of Education regarding the progress of writing the curriculum. Since all curriculum in Kenya is controlled and monitored by the government, the support from the Ministry of Education was crucial to the overall development and success of the project. At the end of the third workshop, the Kenyan leadership team was notified they would be able to meet with the Kenyan Minister of Education and inform him of the overall progress of the peace curriculum. In addition, Eloise and her dean, Linda Samek, were invited to join the delegation to represent the George Fox teams. Eloise and Linda already had an extended stay in Nairobi, so the timing of this meeting they all believed was God given. Needless to say, Eloise and Linda were more than honored they had been asked to join the group to visit the minister.

On the day of the visit to the Minister of Education, Eloise and Linda met with the Quaker leadership team at a predetermined location prior to the meeting in order to discuss what to expect in this unusual invitation. Once the delegation was ushered into the conference room in the minister's office suite, the minister soon joined them in a private conversation. The visit to the Minister of Education lasted just an hour, but within that hour the members of this delegation were able to describe the scope of the project and present the minister with a copy of the most current version of the curriculum. The minister pledged his ongoing support for the project and acknowledged the need for such a curriculum in all of the Kenyan schools. This event highlighted the importance of the relationship building between the two teams since the beginning of the peace curriculum project. If the relations had not been already favorable between the teams, the development of the project would not have progressed as far as it had, and Eloise and Linda would not have been invited to participate in this important meeting. This meeting was not only a humbling opportunity, but a cultural highlight for Eloise and Linda as they recognized the significance of their presence with the delegation. At the conclusion of the meeting, the minister allowed for a photo opportunity with him and the entire group. Both Eloise and Linda still reflect on that photo, realizing not only the significance of that meeting but also how *White* they were in comparison with their Kenyan colleagues and friends. As Linda later reflected about this experience, she shared these insights: "I think about the opportunity to truly be partners with people not like us in so many ways. However, the love of God and others is far stronger than differences that we see." Eloise and John believe that because the principles of cultural humility had been used in the interactions with all of the participants throughout the development of the peace curriculum, this type of meeting with the Minister of Education was indeed made possible.

Once Eloise returned back to the States after that meeting, plans were already in place for word processing the revisions from the third workshop, as well as planning for additional workshops to complete the curriculum for at least Forms 1 and 2 (grades 9 and 10). In the next eighteen months, the development team on a smaller scale held several more workshop sessions, with more revising and editing. Finally, over the course of just two years and six workshop writing sessions on site in Kenya, the development team completed the first edition of the *Curriculum for Peace and Conflict Management*. Now that the curriculum was complete, the next step was for printing all of documents in order to distribute to the Quaker secondary schools. John received information about a possible grant through Philadelphia Yearly Meeting in Pennsylvania, which would help carry the curriculum to this next level. Eloise and John applied for the grant and were awarded $10,000 to assist with the printing and distribution of the curriculum materials. That grant award was the next milestone in this significant project.

The *Curriculum for Peace and Conflict Management*, written for Forms 1 and 2, contains a total of forty-three lessons comprised of eight major themes addressing specific Kenyan cultural needs involving peace and reconciliation concepts in society. Those themes are: 1) Who Am I?; 2) Peace; 3) Virtues that Promote Peace; 4) Conflict and Conflict Management; 5) Life Skills; 6) Human Rights and Responsibilities; 7) Peace and Health; and 8) Peace and the Environment. The primary concepts of the curriculum begin with the theme of Who Am I?, then develop into the themes of valuing one another, diversity as a strength, and the uniqueness and contributions of each individual to school and society.

This peace curriculum, the only one currently of its kind in East Africa, is first and foremost written to meet the cultural and specific needs of students in Kenya. This curriculum also meets the objectives of the first goal of Kenya's National Goals of Education, which states: "*Foster nationalism, patriotism and promote national unity.*"[2]

Kenya's people belong to different ethnic groups, races, and religions, but these differences need not divide them. They must be able to live and interact as Kenyans. It is a paramount duty of education to help the youth acquire this sense of nationhood by removing conflicts and by promoting

2. https://softkenya.com/education/goals-of-education-in-kenya/.

positive attitudes of mutual respect that enable them to live together in harmony, and foster patriotism in order to make a positive contribution to the life of the nation.

At the time the curriculum peace curriculum was developed, the teams also aligned the curriculum with the main components from the "Aims of Peace Education" which were in place at that time:

1. To help learners acquire behavioral knowledge, skills, attitudes, and values necessary to foster behavior that will enhance peaceful co-existence.

2. To empower learners with problem-solving skills.

3. To provide the learners with the necessary skills to be able to solve conflicts.

4. To assist the learners with the skills to promote tolerance for diversity, cultural differences, and human dignity.

5. To equip learners with values and attitudes that promote interdependence and respect of sanctity for human life and appreciation of the environment.

6. To enable learners to promote intrapersonal relationships both at the grassroots, national, and international levels.

In addition to meeting the goals for Kenyan education, the peace curriculum content is also applicable and adaptable for broader Africa. The curriculum consists of three main documents which follow the Kenyan system for curriculum: the Teachers' Guide, Syllabus, and Resource Guide. The forty-three individual lessons from the Teachers' Guide can be used as written, or adapted in any form to meet the needs of a particular school or context. In addition, the curriculum contains recommendations and ideas for extending the concepts into the community and churches. The primary objective is that the peace curriculum is not just for students, but also for teachers, staff, parents and families, and the surrounding communities.

The Resource Guide contains supplementary materials that teachers can utilize to support the written lessons. Or, the teachers can use the syllabus for the goals of the lessons, then use the Resource Guide or other appropriate resources. The curriculum's design allows for multiple strategies to teach the concepts. Most of the information in the Resource Guide was adapted from Kenyan materials or written by selected Kenyan teachers who were involved in the peace curriculum development. The Kenyan planning team first carefully reviewed the supplementary materials, then approved them for adoption into the Resource Guide. Thus, the Resource Guide was also produced by the Kenyans and is culturally appropriate for the unique needs in their schools and country.

The Kenyans initiated the development of this peace curriculum project from the start, with the George Fox team coming along side of them providing the curriculum-design expertise, the word-processing skills, and other technical support. The participating Kenyans for this project provided the key leadership for the main themes, and determined what they believed to be the gaps in peace and conflict-resolution strategies in their school curriculum and communities. In addition, the Kenyan team included the cultural aspects that only they could completely and adequately address. Thus, this curriculum is Kenyan, not written by U.S. educators and given to the Kenyans. From the onset of this project, the George Fox team made the commitment to allow their Kenyan partners to drive the development of this curriculum with the specific components of peace and conflict resolution the Kenyans deemed culturally appropriate. However, the GFU team still sometimes struggled with keeping their pet ideas or concepts out of the way.

During the very first workshop session, one of Eloise's team members came to her in frustration and noted that the Kenyans were not including some key concepts related to peace and conflict resolution. Eloise listened to his concerns, but stood her ground and told him it was imperative to honor the process and allow the Kenyans to include the concepts they believed were most important to their culture. She also reminded this colleague that it was early in the work and the process needed to unfold under the direction of their Kenyan partners. Eloise further advocated that if the George Fox team still noted something was missing later on, they could make general inquiries to see if the Kenyans thought any concepts might have been overlooked. Eloise's colleague agreed with her points and later apologized for asserting his opinions and his Western viewpoint. Not too surprisingly, later on in the process, the Kenyans realized they had missed that very key concept and added it to the curriculum. The important lesson here was that the George Fox team did not *own* the contents of the curriculum; the Kenyans did, since it was their project and they had invited the GFU team into the process. It would not have been appropriate for the GFU team to assert their agenda into the process. Even more important, the contents of the peace curriculum needed to remain entirely culturally relevant to the needs of the Kenyans.

The cultural relevancy of the curriculum remained the highest priority throughout the development of the curriculum, thus honoring the Kenyans and their culture according to the principles of *cultural humility*. Getting the approval of educational leaders in the country was an ongoing effort. Just after the teams had completed the final version of the peace curriculum, Eloise and John, with a copy of the Teachers' Guide in hand, paid a visit to one of the county education officers. When the director saw Eloise, an American, he was somewhat rude in his actions, and his verbal responses indicated he assumed she had brought the curriculum to the Kenyans. Even John was put on the defensive as he reminded the education officer that he had attended informational meetings the year prior and had in fact met Eloise and interacted with her. As the education officer leafed through the curriculum, his tone and overall demeanor quickly changed as John talked through the features of the curriculum, in that it was culturally relevant and written by the Kenyans. At the end of the visit, this education director was highly complimentary of the peace curriculum work and acknowledged he had indeed met with Eloise and the development team the previous year. This was another powerful lesson in the value of the community-initiated and collaborative approach which extended to other stakeholders and policy leaders in the country.

Building the trust between the two groups was critical as both teams navigated this vital project as one unified team. Each participant in this process had to set aside their own personal agenda as all moved forward in the curriculum development. However, by the time the first workshop session came to a close, it was obvious the teams had built a strong bond which would carry them through to completion two years later. God was at work in both groups and it was evident throughout the development of the project.

This strong bond and respect within the development team was evident in several situations. For example, an outside group from another country tried to assert their opinions about the contents of the peace curriculum and voiced their concerns that perhaps the curriculum was not Quaker enough in content. This particular group strongly expressed their opinions to Eloise, who then brought those concerns to the Kenyan leadership team for their consideration. Eloise wanted to be sure everyone was on the same page and that they had not missed a critical opportunity for another viewpoint. However, since this outside group had not built the relationships and trust with the Kenyan team, nor participated in the curriculum development, the Kenyans quickly dismissed the concerns of the group. The Kenyan leaders affirmed the outcome of the curriculum was as originally intended, in that the curriculum could be used for church groups as well as community groups of any religious background, not just Quaker-sponsored schools. Nothing in the content would change. The response of the Kenyan leaders affirmed the message that unsolicited advice would not be accepted from those who had not established trusted relationships with the group. Collegiality, collaboration, and trusted relationships first needed to be built before someone not involved with the project would have the credibility to assert their views or opinions.

Throughout this entire curriculum project, all the principles of cultural humility were used and integrated into all of the work and interactions. That is not to say the George Fox team or the Kenyan team did everything perfectly all of the time. The entire process required give and take on all sides as both groups learned how to work together as one united development team. Both groups intentionally worked on building relationships with each other, and these relationships were carefully nurtured not only in the workshop sessions, but also through the tea times, meals, and social interactions long after the workshops or meetings had ended for the day. The George Fox team was intentional in putting the needs of the Kenyans first in this project and honoring their work and desires for the outcomes. Both teams carefully listened to one another in all areas of the work, by asking questions, clarifying points, and respecting what each person brought to the table in this collaborative effort. The George Fox team quickly had to dismiss any previous assumptions about how quickly they could write the curriculum, or whether they could complete the project at all.

As an example regarding assumptions, a common stereotype is that Kenyans are slow in doing anything. A prevailing expression is, "They are on Kenyan time," referring to people arriving late for an event, or activities beginning late according to Western concepts of time. Because of these stereotypes or assumptions, there were times the GFU team wondered if the project would ever be completed. However, the GFU team decided early on in the process that the peace curriculum project needed to be driven entirely by the Kenyans, and the GFU team would assist as they were able. It was to the great satisfaction of both groups the initial project was completed just two years later after the first meetings and workshops. Not only were the Quaker secondary school leaders motivated to complete the project, they also had a great sense of urgency that this peace curriculum project was desperately needed in their schools and in their country.

Now that the groups had a completed curriculum, the next steps of implementing the curriculum in the Quaker secondary schools would be just as important to the overarching goal of this project: teaching students concepts of peace and conflict management. The components of cultural humility would be just as important in this next phase as with the development of the peace curriculum.

3

Implementation of the Peace Curriculum

THE NEXT PHASE OF the peace curriculum development was now the most critical as the development team considered the best way forward with regards to its implementation. Developing a specialized curriculum such as this without getting it into the hands of the intended recipients would be a tragedy, and potentially demonstrate a lack of respect and recognition for all the time and resources invested in its development. Therefore, the peace curriculum development team needed to create a clear and concrete plan in order to move the project forward into the implementation phase.

The development team, which included John, Eloise, and the Kenyan secondary leadership team, all met together to discuss the main goals and timelines for the implementation process. The Kenyans already knew they could potentially face some challenges and perhaps even some opposition from the Quaker secondary schools. Since the curriculum was a product created under the direction of the Quaker church organization which also provides sponsorship of the Quaker schools, some school leaders believed this was just another mandate forced upon them and ultimately putting them under pressure from the sponsor organization to comply with the request for all Quaker secondary schools to incorporate the curriculum in their schools.

Another potential challenge to implementing the curriculum into the schools was that the daily timeline in the Kenyan schools was already at the maximum with the syllabus requirements in order to prepare for the national exam at the end of Form 4 (grade 12). Further, this curriculum would not be examinable at the national level, so the secondary school leadership team received pushback as to why the peace curriculum lesson should be included in the daily timetables if a test was not required for students. The combined curriculum teams with Eloise and her colleagues, as well as the Kenyan secondary leadership team, continued to address these issues in all of their workshop writing sessions and even after the curriculum was completed. They carefully listened to all of the potential challenges and created strategies to respectfully address the questions and concerns of the secondary school leaders. Forcing compliance of the schools in any way would not model the tenets of cultural humility. As a result, the development team created these initial main goals in order to begin the implementation process:

1. All schools using the curriculum would need to send key leaders to attend specially designed training sessions. The development team believed this point was crucial because they did not want to hand over a set of the curriculum to a school with the potential that it would be placed on a shelf somewhere never to be opened or used. This point was particularly important because the funding for printing and distribution allowed for only one complete set of the curriculum for each school in this initial stage. If participating school leaders attended the training sessions, it was more likely they would become invested in the peace curriculum and ultimately support and adopt it into their schools. More importantly, the development team believed it important for the participants in the training sessions to have the full background knowledge of the history of the peace curriculum development, the overall goals for the peace curriculum, the importance and urgency for the schools, and ultimately, the nation to adopt such a curriculum.

2. The development team also desired to emphasize different strategies for teaching the lessons within the curriculum. Since the written lesson plans contained examples of student-centered methods of instruction, as opposed to the typical and outdated instructional practices of rote learning and lecture methods, the leadership teams wanted to demonstrate to the school leaders different ways they could teach the lessons. It was important for the participants to observe a Kenyan teacher using active and student-centered teaching strategies such as group work, inquiry, and discussions. The development team believed the peer modeling of teaching in the training sessions would be the most effective way to demonstrate the possibilities for teaching

the curriculum and encourage the participants to do likewise. The concepts within the peace curriculum were not developed to produce just head knowledge about the concepts, but to teach students and teachers alike how to incorporate the concepts of peace as a part of one's life, which would then become evident through actions.

3. The development team also desired to allow time for questions about the curriculum. This was another important piece in the entire process which would give a venue for school leaders to voice specific concerns. Representatives from the Quaker secondary schools had participated in the curriculum development, but there were still teachers and principals who did not yet recognize the value of this work, for many different reasons. Having their peers answer specific questions about the content and teaching would assist with the buy-in process from the schools. Since this curriculum was not mandated by the government, the participants needed ideas for how to use precious instructional time to include one more thing—even something as important as this curriculum.

4. The development team also believed it vital to create time to allow participants to share their personal stories about the post-election violence. All members of the development team insisted that this become a priority in the training. The Kenyans did not want to forget that the violence happened in their country, and specific steps were necessary and had to be taken so it would not happen again. As the Kenyan members of the development team shared their own experiences from the violence, it was a somber reminder of how even small differences in opinions or viewpoints could escalate so quickly into full-blown violence. The Kenyans who helped write the curriculum desperately desired that this violence would never happen again and firmly believed in the power of peace education beginning first in the schools, then branching out into every area of life.

The other important part to consider in this implementation phase was that Eloise, as the point person representing George Fox University, would not be in Kenya all of the time to assist with the training sessions. Specific plans would have to be strategically created so that the training would and could continue even in her absence. As the development team planned for the training sessions, Eloise served as more of a moderator, and facilitated questions and clarified specific points, along with helping to organize the final written plan. Because the relationships had been built through the development of the peace curriculum, the trust was already in place to listen and learn from one another as the development team decided on the format for the training sessions.

The development team finally settled on a "train the trainer" process which would utilize selected key teachers and principals as instructors who had been active in the peace curriculum development on a consistent basis. These leaders understood the objectives of the curriculum and could effectively speak to the development of the lessons and content. The *train the trainer* team included mostly members from the curriculum writing sessions. The educational experience levels of these trainers ranged from those newer to the teaching profession (as little four years) to those who had been teaching for many years (up to twenty). Together this team represented a wide range of skills and abilities, which the development team believed was important to the implementation process. The development team also invited several other key stakeholders to join the team who were also members of the Quaker church in Kenya, and well-versed in peace and conflict-resolution efforts.

The development team agreed on a one-day workshop model, and spent an entire day together drafting an outline of each component which would be included for every workshop. This outline would allow for the participants to learn the objectives and main components of the peace curriculum, in addition to engaging with selected content of the curriculum. The development team settled on the following outline for the workshop session:

1. Opening remarks, including welcome, brief history of the project, and what will take place during the day

2. Prayer

3. Ice-breaker activity (to get to know one another)

4. Introductions; self-introductions; name and position at school

5. Purpose of the curriculum:

    a. Definition: The curriculum is a set of formal and non-formal organized instructions for learners, aimed at promoting peaceful coexistence among people as well as the environment.

    b. Discussion: What is peace education?

    c. Activity: Ask the group how the violence affected each of them and their students. Have the group share their experiences with one another and the whole group. Once the discussion is complete, ask the following question: "What can bring harmony to these issues?" Allow responses from the group and write on the board.

    d. What specific measures could have prevented the post-election violence? What about preventative measures today?

6. Syllabus introduction:

    a. Connect the answers to the above question and direct the participants to the syllabus of the peace curriculum.

    b. Have the group take time to read through the content and objectives for Form 1 (grade 9). Allow time for questions or comments from the group.

    c. Have the group now read the content and objectives for Form 2 (grade 10). Allow time for questions or comments from the group.

7. Peace curriculum activities:

    a. The lead trainer for the day selects his or her favorite lesson from the peace curriculum and teaches the entire lesson to the participants.

    b. Group work: The trainer divides the participants into selected groups. The numbers will be determined on how many participants are present. The groups will be instructed to build a lesson using one of the following topics: 1) "Who Am I? Meaning of Self," or 2) "Peace: Ways of Acquiring Peace." The trainer will instruct the participants to build a lesson that is learner centered and creative. The lesson components will include: topic, objectives, content-learner activities, and assessment. The participants will be allowed to use the Teachers' Guide or Resource Guide, but they are to be creative and move beyond what is already printed in the curriculum. At the end of the group session, each group will share what they have created and everyone will discuss and evaluate for the elements of the learner-centered activities, creativity, and relevancy to the peace curriculum.

8. Closing:

    a. Questions and responses from the group

    b. Suggestions

    c. Written feedback

    d. Certificates of participation

    e. Vote of thanks

    f. Closing remarks

    g. Prayer

Once the development team had agreed on the overall structure and assigned the training team their particular duties, they set the date for the first training sessions in consultation with John and his office staff. As the planning continued for the very first training session, John's staff provided the critical support for releasing the information to the schools of each region, arranging for the venues, and carrying out the duties as the host at each session. John's primary role was to identify the schools and mobilize the teachers in those schools so they could participate in the sessions. John also ensured that the necessary resources were in place so the trainings could happen as scheduled. John's role in this effort also contributed to the overall collaboration of this phase. One group could not do it alone—each played a vital part of the entire project.

The participants invited to the very first peace curriculum training session came from Quaker secondary schools in specific regions of western Kenya that had experienced the most violence during 2008. The peace curriculum development team believed these schools should have the first copies of the curriculum in order to begin the implementation as soon as possible. Even though the first training sessions occurred two years after the post-election violence, many of these schools were still in a state of shock and trauma, and existing conflicts had not yet been resolved. As schools were invited to the training sessions, John's office requested that the principal and another key school leader, such as the Head of Studies or deputy principal, attend the sessions together. As Eloise discovered later in her research of the peace curriculum implementation process, the key to successful implementation of the peace curriculum was primarily due to the commitment of the principal.[1] Eloise also found that if the principal was

---

1. Hockett, Examining the Role of the Principal, 23.

not involved or invested in the curriculum, there was either limited or no participation. At one school Eloise and Zadock visited during her research on the implementation, she discovered the principal had not attended the training but sent the deputy principal to represent her and the school. After some probing about what happened to the curriculum copies and the status of the implementation, the deputy principal admitted she had forgotten to tell the principal about the training sessions. Unfortunately for that school and community, all of the peace curriculum materials sat unused on a shelf in a back room for over a year.

The Training Sessions

The first training session for implementing the peace curriculum occurred in the Bungoma area of western Kenya. John and his office staff helped choose this site because it was conveniently located for a large number of schools in the region. John then assisted with selecting two sites in other regions which would be easily accessible for other Quaker schools in those areas. The development team hoped this location strategy would encourage the largest participation possible for the training sessions.

Over forty participants attended the first peace curriculum training session. Most all of the schools participating sent their principal and deputy principal or a head teacher. The peace curriculum training team proceeded as planned in the first training session with the outline they had created. Eloise took careful notes for evaluation purposes once the first training session was completed. The training team also asked the participants to evaluation the workshop at the end of the day. Input from the participants was a vital component in order to make any changes to the structure for the next sessions. This strategy also demonstrated respect for the participants in honoring their perspectives and ideas for the trainers and the development team. After all, the participants would be the ones implementing the curriculum into their schools. John also provided key insights into the training sessions as a participant observer. He was able to engage in the group conversations with the participants and note specific issues or concerns that may not have been brought forth to the entire group. Overall, every person involved with the training session, whether a part of the development team or participant, played an equal role in helping the peace curriculum move forward into successful implementation in the Quaker secondary schools. The inclusive approach to these workshops was an intentional effort for collaboration with all stakeholders in this important initiative. At the end of the first training session when all of the evaluations had been carefully read through in their entirety, the participants indicated they were supportive of the peace curriculum and optimistic about implementing the curriculum into their schools.

One interesting cultural development occurred during the first training session. Since Eloise was in attendance primarily to observe and provide support for the process, the training team kept deferring to her, wanting her to lead the teaching of each section throughout the day. The training team had already agreed on the process and the teaching assignments for the day, but continued to request that Eloise would teach in place of them. She politely declined and encouraged the team to remain with the plan as they had all outlined in preparation for the training sessions, especially since they would be doing future trainings without her in attendance. Eloise later discovered that the training team's request of her to teach was a natural cultural practice to honor the professor who was in attendance, and also an indicator of a lack of self-confidence in comparison with an American professor. Eloise managed to encourage the training team to continue on as planned so they would be confident in carrying out these training sessions after she left the country. This was an area of humility that was difficult to reach, in that Eloise did not want to offend her Kenyan colleagues, but staying on course with the workshop plan was necessary for the intended outcome of creating independence for the Kenya training team, instead of dependency on the Westerner.

After three training sessions for the peace curriculum with Eloise in attendance, and two more sessions carried out by the Kenya team on their own, over one hundred schools had participated and pledged their commitment to this important project. This was a significant first step of moving toward implementing the peace curriculum in all of the Quaker secondary schools.

Peace Curriculum Implementation Follow-Up

The Kenyan peace curriculum development team, along with John and Eloise, determined that a follow-up evaluation plan was also essential to the implementation process. All involved in the development of the peace curriculum desired that this curriculum would become integrated into the distinctive culture of every Quaker secondary school in Kenya. However, the development team also knew that without ongoing encouragement, monitoring, and checking in with the participating schools, momentum could quickly wane away. In addition, many people had invested countless hours of time and energy to create this potentially life-changing curriculum, and all wanted to honor those efforts, knowing the value of the work.

The development team decided to undertake a small research study of the peace curriculum implementation in selected pilot schools one year after the initial training sessions. The overall goal of the evaluation was intended to gauge the level of implementation and commitment of the schools in promoting peace education through the peace curriculum. Eloise took on the role as lead researcher for the evaluation project and partnered with Zadock, one of the Kenyans who had been involved with the peace curriculum work from its inception. The development team agreed it was only natural that Eloise and Zadock should lead this effort since they had the history of the entire project. Furthermore, it was another example of cross-collaborative work in which both would be learning from the other. Zadock would learn the process of qualitative research, and Eloise would further her cultural knowledge and understanding in addition to learning more of the workings of the Quaker secondary schools in Kenya.

Zadock, along with John's advice and input, carefully selected schools for the evaluation they believed would best represent the various types of secondary schools in western Kenya that had participated in the peace curriculum training sessions. It was imperative John and Zadock make this selection since they knew the regions and the schools, and also had full knowledge of the peace curriculum development process from the beginning. After considering all of the schools which had participated in the peace curriculum training the year prior, the following criteria was set for selecting specific schools for the evaluation: 1) leaders from the school had participated in the peace curriculum training the year prior and had a year for the implementation; 2) the school was known to have diverse student populations from a variety of tribes and regions within the country; and 3) the school was representative of each of the six counties in the region. Fourteen schools were finally selected within the following categorizations:

- six mixed day schools
- two girls' boarding/day schools
- two girls' boarding schools
- four boys' boarding schools

The schools selected for this evaluation project also represented the following school categories in Kenya:

- nine district schools, usually day only schools with overall student test scores at lower levels

- four county schools, usually boarding schools only and with more governmental support and higher student test scores at entrance

- one national school, boarding schools only and the highest ranking schools in the country

In order to collect the needed information and data to complete the evaluation, Eloise and Zadock made on-site visits to twelve of the fourteen schools, and interviewed two principals of the remaining selected schools. Both of these principals had also been involved in the development of the peace curriculum project from the initial stage and led the ongoing efforts through the completion of the first edition of the curriculum, the training workshops, and the implementation processes. Prior to each school visit, Zadock contacted the school either the night prior to the visit or the morning of the visit and communicated that he and Eloise were in the area to make a courtesy visit to the school. The intent with the short notice was to hopefully avoid any special preparations for their visit. Other Kenyan leaders involved with this project suggested this strategy in order to create more of a casual and authentic approach as well as a collaborative and non-threatening conversation regarding the peace curriculum implementation. The goal for this approach was to maintain the principles of cultural humility in *learning from the other* within a respectful atmosphere. In no way did Eloise or Zadock desire to create the impression they were out to shame or scold school leaders who had not used the peace curriculum as the development team had intended.

As Eloise and Zadock conducted the school visits, they first had conversations with each principal and at least one more member of the teaching staff, often an assistant principal, chaplain, or another faculty member involved with the peace curriculum work. Each principal readily agreed to share information for research purposes, as well as to help inform others as to effective ways in implementing the peace curriculum. Eloise and Zadock also asked for input regarding improvement to the curriculum itself and the training sessions.

Part of the data collection process also included examining any other evidences related to any kind of peace work in the school or community.

As Eloise and Zadock interviewed the principals and other staff members, they followed an interview protocol for qualitative studies, which asks one question first, then follows up with additional questions as the interview progresses.[2] Using this method, they could probe deeper to facilitate a greater understanding and meaning of the responses. For each interview, Eloise and Zadock asked the initial question: "Describe how your school is implementing or using the peace curriculum."

After each school visit and the interviews, Eloise and Zadock examined the various data they had gathered, debriefed the conversations to confirm the information they both heard and observed, and organized and typed their notes. Through this process, they looked for similar themes, which they then grouped together in order to find specific patterns or trends.[3] Eloise also then shared those data with John for further insight and input into the process. That way they all could make any necessary adjustments into the questioning or school visit strategies.

Based on the data Eloise and Zadock collected, they noticed three distinct levels of implementation of the peace curriculum. They categorized those levels as follows:

- *Minimal implementation*: minor attempt at implementation, perhaps using some lessons from the curriculum through guidance and counseling sessions, and occasional use through guest speakers or other events.

- *Medium implementation*: intentional use of the curriculum through either life skills courses, guidance and counseling sessions, or chaplain's talks; progress in implementation but have not yet made it through the entire curriculum.

- *High implementation*: intentional use of the curriculum through the entire school, creativity in implementation, have trained other teachers to assist with the implementation, have used the entire curriculum, using curriculum as written and suggested for use in the regular school schedule.

In the general analysis of the data, ten of the fourteen schools in this study were implementing the peace curriculum at mostly the medium or high levels. Of the remaining schools, three had made minimal progress

2. Berg, *Qualitative Research Methods*, 80.
3. Creswell, *Qualitative Inquiry and Research Design*, 186.

but had plans in place for full implementation, and the remaining one had dropped the ball entirely and had done nothing. The initial findings showed that the mixed day schools and boys' boarding schools were leading in the levels of implementation. This would now become an area for further exploration as to why these schools implemented the curriculum at a higher level.

One School's Story

One of the schools in the pilot peace curriculum implementation project stood out from all of the others as an overall model for the implementation. Western Friends Secondary Boys' School (named changed for privacy purposes) was intentionally utilizing the peace curriculum as a vehicle to making significant improvements within the school environment, thus earning the label of a flagship school for implementation, and the school was selected for a case study for the peace curriculum evaluation research project.

In order to understand the success of the peace curriculum implementation at Western Friends, it is necessary to examine the state of the school prior to implementing this program into the daily life of the school. When Jonathan (name changed for privacy), the principal of Western, arrived to his post in the middle of the school year several years prior, he found a hostile culture between teachers and students, and a school suffering from prior poor management. Further, neglect of the buildings and property was evident in every corner of the school compound—dormitories were filthy and in need of repair, window panes were either partially or totally missing, and mosquito nets were long gone. Fences surrounding the school were either falling down or missing altogether. Most classrooms had ceilings with water leaks and sagging tiles, along with cracks and large holes in the cement floors. The overall environment was not conducive to effective learning for students or teachers.

At the beginning of Jonathan's tenure at Western Friends, he discovered the school was over US$170,000 in debt to creditors. A new school bus had been purchased the year prior and most of the $71,000 cost had yet to be paid. Jonathan also discovered the school business managers had been misusing a significant portion of the school funds, thus leaving little remaining for even the school's academic operations.

In its early years of existence, Western Friends had been known as a school for academic success, but in more recent years had lost its credibility in the community due to poor leadership. Teachers had become apathetic with their work and absenteeism was commonplace. As a result, the academic curriculum was either not taught or hurriedly reviewed. At the same time the academic performance suffered, the emphasis was placed on the school's football team. Although known for winning many football competitions throughout the region and nation, it was to the detriment of the academic work.

Most of the forty-two tribes of Kenya were represented at Western Friends, and unfortunately, conflicts became the norm. Teachers often argued with one another over a variety of issues and these conflicts spilled out from the teachers' lounge into the classrooms. A lack of discipline was also evident among the student body, with frequent outbursts of violence on the school compound, fights during games and competitions, and students arrested in the community.

The community had lost confidence in the school, resulting in little collaboration between the school and community, apart from the football games. While the school should have been a natural cultural extension of the community, both sides preferred not to associate with the other. Parents from the region tried to avoid sending their young men to the school, unless they were going to play football.

After Jonathan analyzed the issues looming before him, he realized he did not have enough resources in order to make the necessary changes desperately needed at the school. When he heard about the Quaker secondary peace curriculum and training workshops, Jonathan and his newly appointed Head of Teachers, Moses (name also changed), eagerly attended those training sessions. There, both were introduced to the peace curriculum and immediately recognized it as a resource they could utilize to assist with the school's challenges. Through the contents of the curriculum, they hoped that by establishing a culture of peace as a framework for school improvement, the result would be a positive reversal of the dire situations they were facing.

As Jonathan and Moses discussed the peace curriculum and all of the additional resources, they realized that nothing could change unless they first modeled and lived out the basic principles of peace and conflict resolution. When Eloise and Zadock interviewed Jonathan and Moses in the peace curriculum follow-up research, Moses revealed his personal story about how he was a bitter young man, mainly due to the effects and injustices of the post-election violence on his family. As a new and young leader in the school, he was leading out of anger and bitterness, and felt intimidated by the other teachers. Since Moses believed in peace education and its potential for life transformation, he realized he himself must first change in order to move forward with peace in his own life and then with others. Through his own transformation, he would also be able to more effectively lead the teachers through the necessary transitions at the school. This young teacher recognized the need to demonstrate humility first by examining his own attitudes and actions and making those right. Only then could he require the same of anyone else. As a result of Moses' personal commitment to transformation and living it out in all areas of his life, his staff responded positively to his change of attitude and began to support his efforts.

The first step in the school transformation effort was to introduce the entire staff to the peace curriculum. Jonathan and Moses held training sessions to teach the curriculum content, brought guest speakers to the school for added inspiration, and integrated peace education concepts into all aspects of the academic environment. Any teachers not wanting or willing to be included in the school changes were either asked to leave or were transferred. Jonathan and Moses placed the emphasis on all of the staff modeling peaceful behaviors and resolving conflict. In Elavie Ndura-Ouédraogo's work on peace and conflict resolution in the U.S. and the Great Lakes region of Africa, she advocates that for school-wide efforts in peace education, teachers must live out the examples of peace they expect from their students.[4] There can be no other way. In the case of Western Friends, the peace curriculum became a regular part of the school curriculum and was also infused into all student activities. Behavioral issues began to subside and students soon took responsibility for resolving conflicts. In order to resolve the financial issues, Jonathan fired dishonest staff and replaced them with new staff, and prioritized financial issues in order to pay the looming past debts. Jonathan found enough funds to make the necessary school repairs in order to provide a better learning environment for the students. Jonathan and Moses prioritized the culture of peace education and it was soon visible in every area of school life.

Jonathan also recognized that in order for the school to be successful in the transformation efforts, he also needed support and advice from the community. He, along with other school leaders, met with the chief and community elders to devise a plan which would address and hopefully

---

4. Ndura-Ouédraogo, Challenging Quest for Sustainable Peace, 189.

stop the behavioral issues of the students. The chief and elders agreed they would immediately arrest any student sneaking away from school and causing damage or conflict in the community. In this way, the community leaders soon became advocates for the school improvements and brought their wisdom and support to the school leaders. Building on the success of the football team, the school, community, and students worked together to create a healthier environment for the games, thus greatly reducing conflicts during competitions.

In this case study of Western Friends, the peace education curriculum provided the vehicle for successful school improvement. The efforts to integrate peace education throughout the school involved all stakeholders committed to living out the principles of peace. Peace education provided the essential framework leading to "transformative action" while also addressing problems of inequities and injustices among staff and students alike.[5]

Since Jonathan focused his efforts on building a culture of trust and collaboration with his staff, some long-held behaviors within the school and community that negatively affected the students and their academic success were shifted in a positive direction, thus moving the school from a reputation of low academic standards to one of high accountability.[6] The successful transformation at Western Friends can be first attributed to a principal and head teacher demonstrating their own humility as they dedicated their work to incorporate peace education and conflict resolution principles as a vehicle for positive change in the school culture. In addition, they modeled and inspired other school and community leaders to do the same for the sake of their students. For any transformation such as this to continue, it requires humility, trustworthy relationships, collaboration, and an ongoing commitment of strong and focused leadership to make an impact for future students of the school and community. This is an example of cultural humility in action.

5. Ibid., 186.
6. Mulford, Leading Change, 52–53.

4

A Vision for Mt. Elgon

AS ELOISE AND JOHN were working on the peace curriculum with colleagues and other ministry partners, additional educational opportunities emerged from connections to their ongoing collaboration within the Quaker circles. Eloise and John believed these opportunities were the result of successful relationship building and forging strong ties with others, in addition to the collaborative spirit they had developed through their work. As Eloise continued to assist in finalizing the peace curriculum project, John provided vital support and encouragement within his circle of connections through his Africa Ministries Office. Without such strong support, the work Eloise and others were doing could become futile. It cannot be stated enough that a trusted and dedicated partner from the country where one is working remains central to any successful outcomes of an initiative or collaboration. These strong partners are the ones who can provide the critical cultural insights in order to navigate the relationships and connections with key stakeholders.

Mt. Elgon School Initiatives

As John continued with his leadership development work in the various regions of western Kenya, his heart was continually drawn to the communities on Mt. Elgon. This region has had a history of violence even prior to the post-election violence in 2008. Mt. Elgon is a mountain range found between the western side of Kenya and eastern side of Uganda. The same people group lives in this region on both sides of the mountain range. On the Kenyan side live the Sabaots, and on the Ugandan side live the Sabeyis.

The names may look different but these names differentiate between those from Kenya and Uganda. However, they are of the same ethnic group and speak the same language. The population on Mt. Elgon is estimated at 166,088, and according to regional information, approximately 56 percent live in absolute poverty. Seasonal agriculture remains the primary source of income, with limited opportunities for other forms of work. Illiteracy is an ongoing major concern, with the majority of the population barely completing primary school education. Girls are generally not safe in this region, and continue to be exploited by idle men, young and old. Early marriages and childbirth are also prevalent problems. Children are sexually active at a very young age, which produces many instances of diseases, and *babies having babies*. These issues with the girls are primarily due to the continued practice in the region of female genital mutilation (FGM), at which point the girls are then considered of age and marriageable. In addition to the aforementioned issues, the population remains reluctant to trust outsiders, so they tend to keep to themselves.

Other different ethnic groups have gained access on the mountain range since colonialism. Most of the farming land on the range was taken up by the colonial White settlements and pushed the indigenous to the forest, leaving a small part for farming on the Kenyan side. After Kenya gained independence in 1964, people from other communities who had money bought the settlers' farms because the locals could not afford to buy from the White settlers. According to documentation from the local leaders, the communities on Mt. Elgon soon became hostile to any other ethnic group which would attempt to settle on this range. The hostilities even spread into interclan conflicts that resulted in more violence on this mountain range. Some politicians soon formed militia groups in order to gain political mileage on the mountain over the many land injustices that had been experienced in years past, and still continued. As the fighting increased, many people suffered torture under these militia groups that were controlling the mountain range before the government finally stepped in to restore order and respect for humanity.

Young people in this region were especially impacted by the violence, and many young men were forced to flee their homes from the mountain and seek refuge in other areas for fear they would be killed if they did not join either of the militia groups. For those young men who managed to run away, they left their parents in more torture. At most, the fathers of the boys who ran away had their ears chopped off as well as parts of their hands or two fingers. A good number of people lost their lives on the mountain range and many others were also forced into refuge in surrounding areas. Even so, the militia members would still hunt down those runaways and severely torture or execute them if found. When the government eventually stepped up their security, it led to a very high level of death and casualties among the community, which was already bleeding with torture and trauma. Local sources within the region report that approximately six hundred people were killed by the militia known as the Sabaot Land Defence Force (SLDF) between 2005 and 2008, with many others maimed or tortured.

It was within these warring conditions that one of the most notorious militia leaders approached John for assistance. When this leader heard that the government was planning to use the Kenya Defense Force (KDF) to invade the mountain range, he greatly feared for his own life. The leader sent his emissaries to meet with John and Mamai Joseph, the former chairman of Friends Church Peace Team in Kenya. John and Joseph met with the militia leader under very tight security of the militia team of soldiers. The militia leader appealed to John to broker the surrender formula with the Kenya police without killing the militia mercilessly, as the Kenya police had planned. The militia leader warned John that if he dared to betray them to the police, he and his men would wipe out all John's family because the militia knew where John's family all lived. This revelation shocked John, but because of his integrity, which is a key component of the cultural humility approach, John knew he was obliged to seek peace for the many mountain range dwellers, especially since the militia leader sought John's guidance. The militia leader even acknowledged from the beginning of their meeting that the reason he sought out John was because of John's reputation for integrity in his work with others, and his peacemaking efforts throughout Kenya. At the end of their meeting, John promised the militia leader he would try his best to represent their request to the security agents of the government. However, when John made an appointment with the senior police officer commanding the Mt. Elgon region, the military arrived on the mountain and started bombing the hideout of the militia in the rocks on the top mountain. It was now too late for the request of the militia leader to broker a ceasefire and make attempts at peace in the region. John appealed to the police officer to see if they could give the dialogue a chance in order to save many innocent people from dying, but John was told it was too late to stop the attack. John was devastated and felt as if he had personally failed the militia and the people in representing the option of a dialogue in order to voluntarily surrender to police.

It took almost seven months while the military occupied the mountain, and for the residents of the area, the conditions were almost like a concentration camp. Even though the military destroyed the militias from their hiding and the torture from the militia greatly subsided, the armed forces took another twist and created a living hell on earth on the mountain. The soldiers took advantage of the local people and raped women and tortured men they suspected to have been part of the militia. John and many other peacemakers appealed to the government to withdraw the military forces from the community on the Mt. Elgon. The Kenya military finally withdrew and left more harm than the good they thought they came to restore. As a result of the years of war, the number of widows and orphans increased significantly and the people have received virtually no assistance of any kind since the aftermath of the violence. Many of the local leaders have stated that even though there is an absence of war, there really is not true peace since there have not been resolutions to the land clashes, which were the cause of the violence. Since the time the military left the mountain, John has continued to travel throughout the mountain area and engage with the community as he listens to their grievances and identifies himself with them. He has even revealed to many what the militia leader had shared with him before the attack by the military.

One of the great needs in the Mt. Elgon area, which can help to overcome some of the challenges of the past, is for spiritual development through pastoral and lay leader training. Through his traveling within the region and building relationships with the people, John identified a number of young men and women who were spiritually filled and arranged to take them for discipleship training in Uganda for a three-month period. The training was more humbling for John as he saw these men and women not only gain confidence in their personalities, but also courage in their ministry. When this group of men and women returned to Mt. Elgon, they engaged their community in the healing process through the message of Jesus Christ, and especially ministered to those people who live deeper in the forest area at the top of the mountain and are more fearful of outsiders. The newly trained disciples planted new churches in the forest and many people came to be prayed for and eventually joined the Quaker church on the mountain. John later took these same disciples to Friends Theological College (FTC) for further pastoral training. While at FTC, they received more training through the concepts of cultural humility, which have totally transformed them from inside out. These disciples have now trained many other disciples on the mountain and are doing a great work in reaching people for Christ and healing their hearts. Some of those transformed spiritually are boys who were involved in militia groups and had participated in evil activities on the mountain. Within the principles of cultural humility and considering others better than ourselves, there can be total transformation through the blood of Jesus.

Education on Mt. Elgon also suffered during the land clashes and the Kenya post-election violence. For many years, schools on the mountain have been operating under threats of students who were members of the SLDF while at the same time students in the Quaker schools. The students were students during the day and militiamen during the night terrorizing community members. These same students were murderers, rapists, and thieves in the community. During the period at the height of the conflicts, the students threatened the teachers who dared to punish them if they ever did anything wrong in school. Teachers handled them with fear and trembling, and many teachers left teaching and others sought transfers to other schools, but the government denied those requests for transfer. Women teachers ran away because students threatened to rape them.

Chelebei Secondary School, one of the Quaker schools at the top of the mountain, was made as a refugee camp by the community and students who ran away from the other schools in the area. When Eloise and John visited the school with a group of educators, it was the first time John had been to this highest region on Mt. Elgon, and the visitors found the school still in a mourning state three years after the violence had stopped. As Eloise and John met with Moses the principal, a son of the region, he described the immense challenges the school faced. During the land clashes, this region was the epicenter of the violence, with the main gunman coming from the very location at Chelebei. When Moses first came to Chelebei in 2008 after the violence, he found a school mostly destroyed. He reopened the school with thirty-one students, only two teachers, and virtually no supplies. He even had to borrow books for the teachers to use in order to prepare their lessons. In order to reach the school, teachers had to travel to the top of the mountain from the valley below, which becomes even more challenging during the rainy season. The Quaker church in this region has also struggled and up to this point had not provided any support or guidance for the people.

This Chelebei area is also very oppressive for the young women. The practice of FGM is still prevalent, which contributes to a high early pregnancy rate. Many of these girls from the surrounding area do not even complete their high school education due to being forced into early marriages. Girls are still marginalized with regard to education and boys are given more opportunity than girls. At the time of Eloise and John's first visit to Chelebei, the school had a few teen mothers who nursed their babies in the morning, then came to school for their studies. Even though the school had many challenges, the school was making progress and they now had at least enough teachers and textbooks for the students.

As Eloise, John, and the accompanying educators met with Moses, he freely shared with the group that he believed his students were capable of meeting academic expectations if given a chance. He told the educators that most of his students were too poor to even pay the fee to sit for the national exams that year, which came to about $40. One boy in particular was trying to sell cabbage from the family garden plot in order to raise the needed funds. Once Eloise heard that information, her heart was greatly touched with compassion, and she pulled John aside as soon as possible to discuss what could be done for even one student. Moses' words had also impacted John, and he and Eloise conferred as to the possibilities for assistance. However, in this situation, John believed strongly that if they could not help all of the students, then they should not help any of them. All of the students were deserving to sit for the national exams, and excluding any of them would be a tragedy. Yet, Eloise and John did not want to encourage any kind of a dependency just because Westerners were present and visiting the school. However, in this case, John was convinced that assistance would encourage the school and the community leaders, and motivate them to continue support for the school. Finally, John and Eloise came to consensus with a plan. They asked Moses how many students still needed funds to pay for the national exam. Once Moses revealed the number of students who still needed assistance, John and Eloise realized the amount was such that they could find some funds to help pay for the exam fees.

As their time at Chelebei ended and the group prepared to leave, Eloise and John stood with Moses outside in the schoolyard near the front gate. Moses revealed that the spot where they were standing was the epicenter of the land clashes where many people had been killed. Eloise's heart became heavy as she realized the significance of that spot. It was almost surreal to think that the violence had occurred where she was standing. As Moses continued speaking, he stated that peace really did not exist in this region, only the absence of war. Then he challenged Eloise and John with these words: "Climb the hill." He then repeated those words: "Climb the hill." Those were three simple words but they contained a profound challenge. When Moses spoke those words, he did not intend a literal meaning for the location of his school. Rather, his words were a metaphor for getting out of the usual and going beyond. He wanted Eloise and John to look up and envision what the needs and possibilities were in the regions beyond the valley, and how the Quaker church could assist with the rebuilding efforts in the Chelebei region. At the conclusion of their conversation, Eloise and John told Moses they would find a way to pay the rest of the exam fees for the students at Chelebei. Moses was overwhelmed with the news and most grateful for their visit that day. When Eloise and John left Chelebei at the end of the day, their hearts were heavy with all they had seen and heard, but they also had been challenged in ways they had not expected. Somehow Eloise knew she would be involved with more work on Mt. Elgon in the future, but at that point she had no idea as to what doors God might open for further opportunities.

A few months later after the visit to Chelebei, John was notified that one of the female students, who was the most academically successful student, had been taken by an old man for marriage. Moses solicited the services of the local police to retrieve the girl from what had been made her matrimonial home, and they took her back to school to sit for the national exams. This girl was one of the recipients of the funds that paid for her examination fees. Even after not having any formal schooling for over four months prior to the exam, she scored well enough on the exams to qualify for university entrance and actually joined the university for further studies. This particular example illustrates how the concepts of cultural humility have been used in order to transform practices the community formerly embraced. In past practices, girls were mostly seen as less important than boys as far as education and decision making in the community was concerned. As healing in the community continued, they have embraced a different approach which now views girls as having value and in need of further education. The learning through cultural humility still continues.

Education Efforts on Mt. Elgon

Only one year after Eloise's first visit to Mt. Elgon and Chelebei Secondary School, God did indeed open doors for further educational work with the Quaker schools in the region. At that time, the Quaker church sponsored six secondary schools and three primary schools throughout Mt. Elgon. These are the very schools that have suffered from the past land clashes in the region as well as the post-election violence in 2008. At times, principals and teachers from these schools have been able to attend various educational events sponsored by John's office, including the first peace curriculum training sessions. However, logistics of travel and lack of funding have mostly kept these schools isolated from their counterparts in the regions below the mountain. As Eloise was preparing for her sabbatical work in Kenya, John approached the principals of the secondary schools on Mt. Elgon about the possibilities of specifically organizing their schools into their own leadership group. The purpose of such an organization would be to join forces as a united group in order to address the specific and unique needs of these schools in this strife-torn region. Due to the history of violence and turmoil in the area, leaders from the Mt. Elgon schools face many challenges within the school and local communities which principals from other regions have a difficult time understanding. The depth of the issues on the mountain further confirmed the need for a separate organized group for the schools in this area, in order to further the healing process through the young people.

It was within the framework of concern and compassion for these communities on Mt. Elgon that John and Eloise strategized to meet with the school leaders, listen to their challenges, and determine what they needed for assistance in order to improve their schools. Even through all of the challenges they may face, the schools still must educate all students who come through their doors.

Even before John and Eloise would begin any educational work on the mountain, they discussed the principles of cultural humility and how those components should be incorporated into this new initiative with the Quaker schools. Once John and Eloise had agreed on how they would proceed, John contacted the principals of the Quaker secondary schools on Mt. Elgon and invited them to attend a meeting hosted by John and Eloise at one of the secondary schools. At the appointed day and time, representatives from five of the six Quaker secondary schools on Mt. Elgon converged together with Eloise and John, and shared their challenges and specific needs within their schools and surrounding communities. Eloise and John carefully listened to their stories, not wanting to assert any of their own ideas or perspectives upon those who had gathered for this important meeting. As John facilitated the discussions and he and Eloise took copious notes, the principals agreed they needed to organize their schools into their own group on the mountain. Further, they also requested their own workshop sessions which would provide leadership development strategies for their schools in order to address their unique situations. Although the government provides some training for principals, these principals from Mt. Elgon recognized they needed additional support in order to lead their schools successfully in the midst of all of the challenges they faced.

By the time the meeting ended, the principals came to consensus that they wanted to have two days of workshops in which half of their leadership teams would come on one day, and on the second day the other half of the leadership teams would attend. The sessions for the two days would be identical, and dividing the leadership teams in this way would not disrupt the schools and their schedules. The principals' request for including all of their school leadership was also unusual, in that they wanted all of their teachers with leadership positions to attend the workshops so that they could all work together as a team for the benefit of each school. The typical format for a leadership training session is that only the principals and perhaps their assistant principals attend, with the expectation the principal will relay the information to their leadership. Unfortunately, that strategy is not usually effective due to the busy administrative schedules of the principals, and then it can become too easy for information to sit idle, only to be forgotten. In this case, the teachers in the Mt. Elgon schools became collaborators with the principals in order to carry out these new initiatives for leadership development.

The group also set the days, times, and locations for the workshop sessions, with the promise of full support for sending their key leaders to those sessions. One school even donated the use of their bus to go around the mountain to each school and transport the participants to the workshops. Collaboration was clearly evident in all aspects of the planning. John ended the meeting with asking the principals what they needed from him. They were initially surprised at his question but readily provided helpful suggestions. As the principals left at the end of the day, they expressed their gratitude to John and Eloise for the opportunity to form their own alliance, and to engage in such enriching discussions with their peers. Eloise and

John promised to visit the schools as a demonstration of not only their concern, but also their support for the hard work they were doing for the students in their schools. John and Eloise also recognized that the success of the day was the result of intentional prayer, and also allowing the guiding principles of cultural humility to respectfully shape the agenda and conversations. The goal was to ascertain how to meet the needs of the schools on the mountain, and not to shape or assert anyone's personal agenda.

The workshop sessions commenced as scheduled just a few weeks later at Friends Moi High School Kaptama, where the planning meetings had taken place. Several of Eloise's colleagues visiting from the States joined her for this educational endeavor, and they eagerly participated in the planning and delivery of the workshop sessions. The main theme for the sessions was leadership development, and Eloise and her colleagues built on the work of the prophet Nehemiah from the Old Testament and the specific ways he effectively led his people. From the key concepts in Nehemiah, the American educators guided the Kenyans into practical applications for their own schools. Through these sessions, more relationships were forged and nurtured as all the participants shared with one another in discussion groups over tea, at mealtimes, and even into the schoolyard.

At the conclusion of the final teaching session, Eloise and her colleagues had the opportunity to participate in what came to be a delightful cultural interaction. Four boys from the school came to the classroom where the workshop sessions had taken place and requested a meeting with the visitors. These boys, all leaders at the school, desired to take advantage of the presence of the American educators on their campus. Eloise and her colleagues graciously granted the meeting and listened carefully as these young men asked what they needed to do in order to be successful in life. The boys also inquired about the role and work of a professor. The final question was perhaps the most important, as they wanted to know how best to spiritually encourage their classmates. After about twenty minutes of interactions, the principal indicated the boys had taken enough of the visitors' time. Before the young men left, Eloise asked them if she could pray for them. As Eloise finished her prayer and looked up, unbeknownst to her and her colleagues, a group of men had gathered behind the boys and had entered into that holy space of conversation and prayer. John had observed the interactions with the boys and affirmed that God was indeed at work on the mountain.

A few weeks after the first workshop sessions on Mt. Elgon, Eloise and her Kenyan colleague Zadock visited five of the Quaker secondary schools on Mt. Elgon which had participated in the workshop sessions. The objective was not just to fulfill the promise to visit the schools, but rather to further the relationship-building process through engaging with the school personnel and students, in addition to careful listening to the needs and challenges each school faced. As Eloise has previously noted, she has difficulty grasping the concept that what might seem to her as a simple and courteous school visit can positively impact that school for many years as they recount the historical record of a visit from an American professor. That is a concept often not fully understood from a Western perspective. The school visits were not only informative, but revealed the depth of the needs and challenges for the schools on Mt. Elgon. Steps were already in place to help the schools move forward with effective leadership strategies in order to address academic issues and other challenges, but unfortunately the needs were great and resources few.

Not long after the workshop sessions, Eloise was presented with another opportunity to assist with the school efforts on Mt. Elgon. The principal from Friends Moi High School Kaptama contacted John and invited him to be the main motivational speaker for the school's annual Day of Prayer. John was not available for that day, but after the two men consulted, they agreed Eloise should be the speaker instead of John. Further, they reasoned that Eloise speaking at this event would be a natural extension of the work she was already involved with in the area. When John presented this invitation to Eloise, she was shocked, but also immediately anxious about what would be required of her for this event. She did not accept the invitation until several days later after she and John discussed the expectations. Although Eloise had already spoken at churches and other meetings, and delivered professional development at quite a number of Kenyan schools, this was one event she had not personally experienced and therefore had no knowledge of the context. John described that this event consisted of a day-long program with special speakers to motivate and encourage the candidates (grade twelve students) who were about to sit for their national examinations. The results of these examinations would potentially determine the students' next steps in life. After prayer and consideration, Eloise believed God would give her the right message to share with the candidates and the community, but in her soft-spoken style, totally opposite to John's exhortational and motivational speaking style. Cultural humility ultimately played a role in her decision to accept the invitation as she considered that accepting would further the relationship building within the community, and continue to build on the efforts they had experienced in recent weeks with the workshop sessions and school visits.

John assisted in preparing Eloise for the expectations of the Day of Prayer, and together they worked out a sermon outline with a Scripture text John affirmed as appropriate and timely for the candidates and the community. As the time came for the Day of Prayer at Friends Moi High School Kaptama, Zadock accompanied Eloise to the school and they participated in the scheduled program. Eloise found the entire event quite fascinating and another learning opportunity to fully engage with the cultural practices of this area. The main building used for large events, such as church services and other programs, was completely filled with the candidates sitting on the hard benches, other students sitting behind them, and honored guests and teachers seated in the front. Community members filled the spots outside as close to the building as possible in order to view some of the guests and proceedings. A loudspeaker ensured that guests for miles around would be able to hear the entire program. Eloise soon discovered that the main motivational speaker was scheduled at the conclusion of the program. By the time she was next to speak, the students had already endured over four hours on those hard benches listening to various speeches from teachers, local pastors, and education officials. Right before she was introduced, Zadock wisely suggested that everyone take a standing break for a few minutes in order to prepare for Eloise's message. When the participants were finally seated and she took the front of the stage area, the candidates suddenly sat at their tallest and brought out their notebooks and pencils. Zadock later told her, "Prof, it was you they wanted to hear." Eloise delivered her message, first using the passages of Scripture from Matthew 5:9, "Blessed are the peacemakers, for they will be called children of God," and Hebrews 12:14, "Pursue peace with everyone, and the holiness without which no one will see the Lord." Utilizing these passages as the foundation for her message, Eloise also incorporated the main Quaker values of peace, integrity, equality, and simplicity. It was the message of peace that was so desperately needed in this region. Eloise reminded the candidates that it was their responsibility as future leaders to lead the community into peace and conflict resolution. After Eloise concluded her message and sat down, she knew without a doubt she had made the right decision to accept the invitation to speak to the candidates. It was evident the spirit of God was present with her and through her message. After the final prayer and all of the participants were dismissed, a very tall, thin, and older gentleman walked up to her to shake her hand. He introduced himself as the chief of the Kaptama region. As they engaged in discussion, his final words will be forever etched in Eloise's mind and heart: "Professor, thank you for your words. You have given me something to think about today." Then he slowly turned and left. God was indeed working on the mountain that day and Eloise, John, and other leaders were encouraged with the fruit of their labor.

5

Friends Theological College and Connections to Communities

FRIENDS THEOLOGICAL COLLEGE (FTC) in Kenya was established in 1942 for the purpose of training pastors and lay leaders in East Africa at a time when the Quaker church was rapidly spreading through the efforts of missionaries who had been sent to the region. Friends Theological College is located within ethnic communities that have been at conflict with each other for several years, especially after the original East Africa Yearly Meeting was split into several yearly meetings. After the split, the college remained a center of reconciliation with a focus on cultural humility, through which the teachers and administration of the college promoted and facilitated the approach of how best to work together despite the differences in communities.

The principles of cultural humility were inculcated into the pastoral training at the college, and this saw the transformational approach of the students who went out into the communities to carry out their ministry. These students helped model Christ's approach in accepting and respecting each other's culture in the communities they served. It was during this time the church leaders realized how important the college is in the modeling of humbly respecting another irrespective of their ethnic group.

FTC is a center that lives out cultural humility naturally through a process that has been assimilated into the teaching and learning of pastoral development. The training itself has cultural humility as its natural foundation, and pastoral transformation has been evident as the church leaders see these students help communities come together and work in harmony. It is through the efforts of FTC and the focus on cultural humility that surrounding communities can see the growth of unity and harmony in the churches throughout East Africa. The college has seen itself at one point even having both the Hutu and Tutsi members from Rwanda in the college, and they all worked together. In addition, the learning environment at FTC promotes peace building through cultural humility not only among the students and staff, but also in preparation for life outside the college.

The Quaker church has adopted an approach of cultural humility in the ways they reach various communities with ministry practices that promote equality and respect for others. This has led to the church in Kenya growing fast because of cultural humility in ministry among the many different ethnic groups in the country. The rise of cultural diversity among Quakers in this region can also be attributed to the training at FTC. These pastors and lay people who have been trained at FTC continue to be involved in various pastoral and reconciliation efforts across East Africa, and because of the cultural humility approach, the evidence is the beginning of harmony in these communities.

Cultural humility, especially within the framework of pastoral training, is unique and respectful in its own way. In learning how to better relate to others, people change and adopt a friendlier, peaceful, appreciative, and all-inclusive way of living, without realizing they are doing so. This is the same spirit from Jesus' method of how he raised up his disciples. Jesus, a carpenter and not a fisherman, approached the fishermen after they experienced an entire night of fishing without success. It was midday and the men were very busy cleaning and mending their nets in readiness for the next round of fishing in the night. Jesus jumped into one of the boats that belonged to Simon Peter and the brothers. Jesus started preaching from the boat to this group of fishermen who were all busy cleaning their nets on the shore. In this way, Jesus identified himself with the fishermen on the seashore. He later requested Simon Peter and his team to go back that day to the deeper part of the sea and launch their nets into those waters. It was difficult for those men to go fishing in the scorching sun because the fish are not easily found on the surface of the sea, but in deeper waters where nets often cannot reach. These men had been practicing the traditions of fishing as learned from their fathers and could not imagine another way of doing things. The men argued with Jesus and tried to reason with him as to why it would not be easy to catch fish during such a time. Since Jesus had already identified with them, he was able to convince them to follow his instructions. They conceded to his request and left for the deep sea with their fishing tools on their boat. As Jesus connected with these men through the approach of cultural humility, the result was a powerful and surprising result never before witnessed or expected.

After the men launched their nets into the sea, the nets started sinking deeper. When the men started pulling the nets toward the boat, they discovered the nets were full of fish and they could not manage to get all the fish to their boat. The nets were much too heavy for the men and they had to call on their friends from the shore to come and help them, for their boat was almost sinking. Others came with their boats and they also filled them and arrived on the shore with the boats full of fish at an odd time of the day. All who witnessed these events were amazed and surprised with the fish harvest which they had never experienced before in their fishing career. This convinced Simon Peter and his siblings that Jesus was not just an ordinary human being. When the men were asked to follow Jesus and stop fishing for fish and start fishing for people, the men followed Jesus without question and left the fishing career they had known all of their lives (Luke 5:1–7). Cultural humility is a spiritual disposition that does not force one to do things, but humbles one to take action without doubt, and hence connects with strangers very well. Through Jesus' modeling of cultural humility and building respectful relationships with Peter, James, and John, their lives were transformed from being fishers of fish to fishers of men.

An integral part to effective pastoral training at any institution is through qualified and dedicated faculty. One of the ways Eloise has been involved in FTC is through the training of the faculty, who are responsible for teaching and preparing the students who come through their doors. As the institution was preparing for their accreditation requirements, the faculty identified specific areas for assistance in effective teaching strategies, and invited Eloise to lead workshop sessions with those topics. Since many of the faculty at FTC tend to be either pastors or specialists in a theological content area, they often lack the expertise or knowledge on effective teaching skills. These skills are necessary not only to improve the learning for their students, but also to meet the diverse needs of the learners at their institution. As Eloise acquired more knowledge about the institution and their specific needs for their faculty and students, she prepared materials that focused on the needs of adult learners, and how to adjust one's teaching to meet the educational aspects for all of their students. Since students from other African countries were attending FTC, their background and learning requirements were different from the students who had been schooled in Kenya, and it was important to consider the unique needs of everyone.

As Eloise has found in her own teaching and research, one of the key components of working with adult learners is through relevancy of the content. Most adult learners from any background have a desire to know and understand the context of the material, take charge of their learning, and make meaning from their own initiatives.[1] Further, adult learners require a structure in which they can continue to build upon basic learning concepts while making immediate application to real-life situations. Therefore, relevancy of the course content is necessary and of value to adult learners in order for them to make the appropriate connections of past events and experiences and relate them to current concepts. It would be important then for the instructor of adult learners to provide the necessary collaborative and relational framework in order for the learners to explore new learning concepts, thus helping to insure a successful learning opportunity.[2] The components of cultural humility, especially within the context of relationship building and following the example of Christ's humility, also provide the necessary framework, then, in which to teach all adult learners from all backgrounds in order to prepare them to meet the needs of various people groups. This type of teaching framework is especially important for instructors who are teaching pastors and lay leaders in order to prepare and effectively equip them for the ministry roles in the various communities God calls them to serve.

Eloise considers it a distinct honor to have facilitated several professional development sessions for the FTC faculty in recent years. These sessions have provided valuable insights not only to Eloise, but also to the faculty as they share together and relay information about their students and various cultural practices which are vital to learning about cross-cultural ministry in Africa. The faculty have also invited Eloise to observe their classes and help them reflect on their teaching practices and have her offer suggestions for improvement. These observations have also provided Eloise additional information on many cultural aspects related to the teaching and learning process at FTC.

Eloise has appreciated the dedication of the faculty at FTC, and recounted several interesting interactions with the faculty related to the workshops she has provided for them. Some months after the first workshop

---

1. Knowles et al., *Adult Learner*, 62–69.
2. Cercone, Characteristics of Adult Learners, 159; Vella, *Learning to Listen*, 52.

session Eloise delivered, she encountered several faculty at a church function in Kenya. These faculty members shared with her how excited they were that they were able to teach the concepts Eloise had taught them to faculty from other colleges at a recent conference. They were almost boasting they had such knowledge and the faculty from other institutions did not. When Eloise returned for another workshop several years later, she found almost the same participants as before, plus a few others. What surprised her most, however, was that the faculty recalled exactly what she had taught them in the first session and how they continued to use those concepts in their courses. Another faculty member went on to report that she incorporated some of the information from Eloise's first workshop into her thesis for her master's degree. These are the types of interactions that motivate Eloise to continue her work in Kenya wherever God calls her. John believes that Eloise's professional development work has impacted changes in building the cultural humility approach through the faculty and then onto their students.

One key aspect of John's ministry in Kenya and East Africa is to provide discipleship training, and prepare future leaders to grow and expand the Quaker church throughout Africa. As he works with church leaders, he has recognized the need for Kenyan missionaries to be sent out to other countries, or to bring students from other countries to be trained and then sent back to their communities. John is committed to identifying students from Tanzania, Uganda, the Democratic Republic of the Congo (DRC), and different communities within Kenya, and bringing them to FTC for pastoral training. This is especially urgent when the church is opening a new ministry in a different community in those countries or within Kenya. Especially within this context, cultural humility virtues are needed, and hence building leadership that reaches the communities with this approach. The Quakers have realized many new churches in communities in Tanzania and the DRC through the training programs at FTC.

Through the training at FTC, students from these many different backgrounds and cultures learn how to respectfully engage with others even with differences in theology. One example of this learning centers on the Quaker position on baptism. The Quaker church emphasizes the baptism of the Holy Spirit in one's life, and less of the outward practice of water baptism, believing in the internal change of the person that is then reflected and evident from the outside. This concept of inward baptism is not easily understood by many, especially those from other areas or denominations where the practice of water baptism is the only way one knows how people are baptized. How then is cultural humility evident through this difference in belief?

John and other leaders have witnessed the change from these students after going through training that opens their inner understanding of the Quaker baptism. As they learned through the concept of cultural humility in respecting others, the students have acknowledged and accepted the Quaker teachings of the inner baptism of the Holy Spirit. The church leaders have seen these same students go back to their countries and teach the same concepts using the framework of cultural humility. The result has been one of the most powerful means of spiritual transformation. This has seen cultural humility as the most effective spiritual influence that totally transforms people's lives permanently from change within the inner self which others can see from outside. It is a practice that sees one respecting another person and views them from the inner perspective as an equal and appreciated creature as he/she examines themselves spiritually. Cultural humility can transform one who despises others to a total change of heart in appreciating everybody. It is the most effective spiritual transformation from one belief that was self-centered to embracing the possibility of faith in accepting each other.

One example of John's efforts with leadership development with other countries has been with students he brought to the college from the Democratic Republic of the Congo. As these students progressed in their studies and pastoral training, John was able to personally observe the transformation in their lives. When those students returned to their communities in the DRC at the conclusion of their studies at FTC, they opened many Quaker churches in eastern Congo and the church there began to grow and flourish. When John visited their churches in the DRC, he was amazed to see how the principles of cultural humility helped them start many churches by first understanding each community, then helping the same community recognize the need for a church to be planted there.

John believes the main description of his organization's mission appropriately describes the outcomes of his ministry: "Jesus Christ, a simple faith that transforms lives." It is within this simple faith that John saw a group of soldiers in the DRC join one of the churches in a rural area. These soldiers were living in the forest trying to fight the rebels in the region, and one day they experienced Christ's humility and transformation for themselves. As John was ministering in the DRC, he experienced one of the shocks of his life. He had finished preaching his sermon about peace and how Jesus is the prince of peace, and all who embrace Jesus have a stake in this peace. Immediately after John's message and before he prayed, a military commander walked up to where John was standing, and the man's presence almost shook John to his core. John wondered what he might have done, but continued to smile at the commander as he moved closer to him. The commander stood just several feet away from John and questioned him, "Why has it taken all this long for you to come here and preach this powerful transforming message? If you had been here before preaching this message, we would not be in this situation we are in now!" The commander whistled for his soldiers to come closer, and a swarm of them came out from under the bush where they had been listening to John's message. The commander demanded that John pray for them and wish them protection, and promised they would join John and his team the following day for another service. From that moment, they were members of the Friends church and they disappeared back into the bush. Under their commander, these soldiers asked John and the local church leaders to open as many churches as possible because they saw the presence of peace in the churches and believed that this Jesus who John and others preached about was truly a model for peace. This was an incredible example of how the aspects of cultural humility through the message of Christ's peace touched the hearts of those soldiers and helped them change their course of action. It also highlights a great need for additional disciples and leaders to bring the message of Jesus Christ to the DRC.

John's ongoing commitment to expanding the Quaker church throughout East Africa has also presented ministry opportunities in Uganda. John and Eloise had the occasion to visit Uganda together with leaders from Wabash Friends Church in Indiana, U.S. The purpose of the visit was to discern together with Uganda Friends Church leaders how John and other partners could collaborate in mission work with the Quaker church leaders in Uganda. The principles of cultural humility were employed in this effort so that, together, John and the Ugandan leaders of the Quaker church could consider developing leadership concepts from what they knew, as well as learning what they did not know. As John, Eloise, and the other members of the team met with the church leaders, they did not take the approach of traveling to Uganda to show them how leadership should be done. Rather, the team sat and listened to these leaders in order to learn what they knew about leadership and needed, and what possibilities there might be to assist and come alongside them in ministry and leadership development. The

Quaker church in this region was just in its infancy due to the past wars and conflict in Uganda, and the needs of these leaders were different from the Quaker church in Kenya. These leaders articulated a need for their own administration building which would validate their church organizational structure to the government. The Ugandan church leaders believed they needed this structure prior to beginning any leadership training. Had John and the team made assumptions of what these leaders needed, they could not have guessed their request for such a structure. These listening sessions became vital to the future development of the Quaker church in Uganda. This same approach was later followed by FTC using the same leadership development process whereby the local leadership would adopt the same effective leadership practices that had seen the Ugandan Friends Church make progress in their leadership development.

The growth of the Quaker church in Tanzania is another example of how leadership training at FTC has directly benefitted the churches in that country. Cultural humility has transformed many pastors from Tanzania who were trained at FTC and are now managing churches in Mwanza and other parts of Tanzania. It is through the cultural humility framework that they are able to pastor in communities that once could not accept Christianity. However, due to the tenets of cultural humility which show respect to the other cultures and approach them from building an understanding of the communities, people are coming to Christ and new churches are being established. John and other leaders of the Quaker church are pleased that this approach has seen the churches opened across borders of Tanzania and Malawi, in addition to Tanzania and Zambia. This is just another example of how cultural humility is an effective tool for the outreach ministries to other cultures.

The Kenyan Quaker church has been embedded in a complex ethnic conflict over the leadership of the churches. FTC has become a remedy for the unity through the cultural humility process. Leaders from Tanzania, Uganda, Kenya, Rwanda, and Burundi have been involved in cultural humility training through the FTC leadership training program. Most people are fully aware of the genocide that took place in Rwanda in 1994, the post-election violence that shook Kenya in 2008, and the internal conflicts in Uganda and its churches. All of these wars and conflicts were due to cultural differences that the communities experienced. When one feels pressured or challenged, the reaction is often violence leading to death. FTC is modeling a strong framework of cultural humility that helps all who come to the college from these different communities learn how to work together and appreciate one another as an important part of the community at FTC and within the global church. FTC is now the hub of incorporating the concepts cultural humility within its training programs, and the outcome is strengthening the Quaker church in the Eastern and Central African regions.

6

Musembe School

How One School and Surrounding Community was Transformed

THE STORY OF ELOISE and John's work in the Muliro Village area of rural Kenya perhaps best represents all of the tenets of cultural humility in play at the same time. Eloise and John had the unique opportunity to enter into a project that had not been on their radar, nor one they had envisioned or planned for. However, God had specific plans for one small primary school known as Musembe, and the surrounding community of Muliro Village.

In Eloise's previous visits to Kenya, she had the opportunity to visit the Muhanji farm and observe and follow the building progress of the house and other structures. Once the family had moved onto the site, Eloise had the privilege of spending two weeks on the farm during her sabbatical from George Fox. During this sabbatical time, Eloise rested mentally, emotionally, and physically, visited with family and community members, and observed the daily rhythm of community life in the village.

Every time Eloise had visited the farm, even before John and his family moved there, she was always told the sad story of the Musembe primary school, its lowest place academically in the entire nation at one point, and the disdain the community had for the school. It was not until John moved into the Musembe neighborhood that concerns of the school were raised out of his personal convictions of having his own children in higher-learning institutions. This would never be a dream seen by the children from this community. However, since the school was sponsored by another church group and not a Quaker school under John's organization, John was at first reluctant to interfere with the work of the other denomination. And yet, children from the surrounding community attended this school in his very neighborhood; children who would grow up to be members of this community and have families; children who would still be entrenched in the cycle of poverty and mostly uneducated.

One morning during Eloise's sabbatical stay as John was driving her into town for business and errands, they drove past the school once again and Eloise's burden for this school became too much for her to bear. Eloise recalls that her heart finally broke over the extreme needs of the school and she knew God was speaking to her about her possible involvement. Initially, she was reticent to become involved since she usually worked with secondary schools, but the burden was too great and she knew she must do something. As John drove up the hill past the school, Eloise blurted out to him, "Who is going to care for these children and how will they receive a chance for a decent education and opportunity at a better life if someone doesn't help them"? Eloise continued to pour out her heart and John intently listened to Eloise's burden for the school. When Eloise finally stopped speaking, John responded that he had been convicted of his negative attitude toward the school and had planned to talk to Eloise about what to do regarding Musembe. However, as Eloise acknowledged in their discussions, she and John were already so busy with many other things. It was within those words that both Eloise and John realized they needed to make time for the *least of these*. Responding to the burden God had placed on their hearts, Eloise and John began the effort to consider what could be done for such hopeless children whose choice is not to be who they are.

Musembe Pentecostal Assemblies of God (PAG) Primary School is located in Bungoma County, a subcounty of Tongaren in Ndalu. The school is built along the border of Trans Nzoia County and draws its students from the slums in the county. Most of these families are headed by single mothers, some who are widows or divorced, while others have never been married. Some of these women are local brewers of illegal beer in order to support themselves and their families. Often times, girls from the school are required to help make the brew during the night, thus impacting their time for their studies and ability to remain awake in school during the day. In the process of these illegal activities, the mothers have children out of wedlock and raise them without fathers. Still, other women are practicing prostitution to feed their children, with some even selling their daughters as young as twelve to older men in order to make money.

The population in the Musembe area has not been well documented, but it is estimated that ten thousand people live in the neighboring slum, and the Musembe neighborhood, which is the catchment area for the school, has a population of three thousand. The majority of the population tend to be middle to younger-aged people, with a general life expectancy of approximately fifty years. Children from the homes in this region have hardly any hope of going for future studies beyond their time at the Musembe primary school. The word *Musembe* actually means "tail." At one point, the children even knew of themselves as the "tails" of other schools.

The community's main economic activities center in agriculture, and since the majority of the parents do not own land, they make their living by contracting for work on other people's farms during harvest times. The pay for this type of menial labor is usually only worth a day's meal. A high rate of HIV remains prevalent in the slums and most of the children end up staying with their infected parents or guardians, and some of the children are even infected as well. The community is completely backward in terms of education and technology. However, the government has recently supplied the Musembe school with power, with the commitment that all schools in the country should have a power supply in order to progress with educational initiatives.

As Eloise and John discussed their options for any kind of involvement and helping the school, they knew that it was a delicate situation and they would need to proceed carefully. They first discussed the principles of cultural humility within the context of the needs of the school and community. Eloise and John had also read and discussed many related publications on international mission endeavors, and were determined not to enter into a new work and create any kind of a dependency or specific efforts that were not going to be welcomed, viable, or sustainable in the community. Eloise and John also knew they could not just march into the school to take over and force the leaders to let Eloise and John help them. Forcing their way into the school even with the honorable intention of helping would totally violate the principles of cultural humility in which they so strongly believed. The projects Eloise and John were already involved with had been informed by the main tenets of cultural humility, and they firmly believed in cultural humility as the guiding principle for any work they were currently involved with or would undertake in the future. However, Eloise and John also recognized that the burden for this particular school was divinely inspired, and they knew they had to make a concerted effort to assist in some way, no matter if the effort was small or large. The remaining question was, how?

Outsiders

One of the key issues Eloise and John recognized and wrestled with from the beginning was that they were both outsiders within this context in Muliro Village. As strange as it may seem, John was an outsider even though he was Kenyan, had bought land in Muliro Village, moved into the community, and already knew many people in the region. Eloise was even more of an outsider because she was a highly educated White woman from America—*mzungu* (White person). In Andrea Nelson's dissertation research of Kenyan principals from Quaker secondary schools, she found that one of the challenges of the principals she interviewed was that they were considered outsiders when they were assigned to a school in different regions of the country and among different tribal groups. In Andrea's study, the principals reported that being outsiders often limited their work within the community until they were able to build relationships and trust with the community members. Just because one was Kenyan did not mean there was automatic acceptance within another community. Those relationships still needed to be intentionally built and carefully nurtured.[1]

As Eloise and John continued to discuss possible strategies for Musembe, they finally decided that as a first step they would arrange a meeting with the school leaders at the Musembe school site. Eloise and John believed an introductory meeting would be the most natural way to begin any relationship-building process with the school leaders and teachers, and also gauge if the school was interested in or desired any kind of assistance from people within the community or outside. As Eloise and John were discussing the most practical way to proceed even with a first meeting, it just so happened Eloise was going to have visitors in Kenya while she was on sabbatical, and Eloise and John believed it was timely that these colleagues would be arriving to visit so they could begin their time in Kenya with a visit to the Musembe school. The first day Eloise's George Fox colleagues were in Kenya, John arranged for an afternoon meeting at the school with the teachers and the U.S. visitors: Linda Samek, her dean; and Andrea Nelson, her doctoral student.

---

1. Nelson, Knowing How to "Engage" Cross-Culturally, 82.

John, Eloise, and her colleagues first met with the teachers in their humble teachers' room, a mud structure with hardly enough space to turn around in, and barely enough square footage for a long table with chairs around for all of them to be seated. The deputy principal and John facilitated the visit, and all in attendance awkwardly proceeded with formal introductions. Once the introductions had taken place, the visitors were ushered outside and treated to a traditional welcome, which included a *parade* (assembly) with the students, teachers, and community members. As per custom in most Kenyan schools, several of the children's groups had prepared traditional cultural dramas and musical numbers for the visitors. After the assembly concluded and the children were sent home, the meeting with the teachers and staff resumed. John and Eloise first shared their desire to engage in some kind of partnership and inquired as to what the school needed. This was the first of the questions that represent a key component of cultural humility, specifically asking about the current needs. However, at this initial meeting the teachers were neither able nor ready to articulate specific needs, let alone any needs at all. As Eloise and John later discovered, while the teachers were grateful for the visit, they were too demoralized and overwhelmed in their work, and therefore did not have the emotional capacity to even know how to respond to the inquiries about needs at the school. Eloise and John concluded the meeting with praying for the teachers and the school, and then promised they would remain in touch. As John finished praying, several of the women teachers sitting in the back of the room were silently crying. As Eloise and her colleagues prepared to leave the school, they took a group photo with the teachers to commemorate this visit.

Eloise and John did not find out until a few years later the reason for the tears of those women. One of the women, Jane, had been at the school for over ten years, quietly laboring for the students the best she knew how, and praying for someone to come and provide assistance. Another teacher, also called Jane, had been assigned to the school just two years prior to Eloise and John's first visit. As Jane reported for duty and found the school in such a sad state of affairs, she prayed for God's intervention. As Jane later told Eloise this story, she relayed the following information: "I told my students that we must pray because God was close and was going to bring us someone to help." At the end of Eloise and John's first visit to the school, teacher Jane already believed God had just answered her prayers.

As Eloise drove off with her colleagues that day after their Muembe visit, Linda remarked, "What are we going to do about this school?" Nobody had an answer to that question, but Eloise and John believed there was now a beginning. As Eloise wrote later in her journal, she felt dismayed that, in her assessment of the meeting, nothing was accomplished at all, or nothing that she could outwardly see. No decisions were made, no plans were made, and nothing concrete happened. However, as Eloise and John reflected on this first visit, it was the first step in establishing a relationship with the school, no matter what that relationship might ultimately look like.

The first lesson learned with this school was that a beginning point was necessary, and Eloise and John would have to be patient to see how that beginning would unfold and lead them into further interactions with the school personnel. Since God had clearly spoken to Eloise and John about the needs of the Musembe school, her initial personal expectations assumed that she and John would immediately embark on a project and get going. Not so. This effort was going to take time, and they needed to let God direct their steps at each stage and be patient with the timing. This was also an area in which Eloise needed to carefully and cautiously examine her own motives and her Western perspective of desiring quick outcomes to a project. John kept encouraging Eloise that they had to take a wait-and-see approach and could not force anything with the school. John would also need to continue relationship building within the larger community in order to garner their trust. The principles of cultural humility also include the attitudes of humility and patience, and to take time as one engages in the initial relationship-building process. Even though John and Eloise believed their burden was real and that God wanted them to do at least something at Musembe, they recognized the important lesson of waiting for God's specific directions. As Eloise left the village at the end of that first visit to accompany her visitors for the educational work for which they had come to Kenya, her heart stayed behind at that little forgotten and forlorn school at the end of the mud road close to the river.

A few weeks after that first visit to Musembe, Eloise returned to the village once more before she was scheduled to return to the U.S. Eloise had requested to visit Musembe again, but this time John's wife, Rose, made the arrangements and accompanied her. Eloise had wanted to be more active in the school since it was a part of the community, and this would provide her an opportunity to meet with the teachers within their professional environment instead of just greeting as they passed on the road. As Eloise and Rose were ushered into the cramped and dark teachers' room and sat around the wood table, they reiterated the theme of the previous visit: that they had come to see what the school needed, and how they could be of help. Once again the visit did not seem to produce any fruit, and Eloise and Rose left with feelings of frustration. For one thing, nobody at the school had offered them anything to drink during the visit, which was a major cultural oversight, and Rose was appalled at this lack of hospitality. Secondly, the teachers seemed reluctant to engage in conversation and answer Eloise and Rose's questions, which prompted Eloise and Rose to wonder why the teachers were holding back. It is difficult for one to listen and learn the needs of others if the conversation is one-sided. As Eloise and Rose were about to leave, they were told that the teachers did not recognize Eloise when she arrived with Rose. When Rose asked the teachers why, they stated it was because there were more White people on the previous visit and they looked the same. However, upon further discussions with the teachers a few years later, they explained that the first visit was mainly an encounter with the entire group, with limited interactions among each individual. The relationship-building attempts during the first visit had barely scratched the surface for name and face recognition. This is another example that relationship building with others requires ongoing and consistent efforts. However, Eloise and Rose acknowledged once again that relationship building can take time and they were committed to the process, as well as engaging others in the community about how to help the school. Furthermore, Eloise also needed time to become a student and learn the culture of this village and its little school.

When Eloise's scheduled time in Kenya ended, she went back home and continued to reflect on that little school seemingly in the middle of nowhere, among the cornfields of rural Kenya. She tried to process those visits to the school, and continued discussions with John about what could be done and how they should proceed. All through Eloise and John's discussions, they agreed they would follow the principles of cultural humility and wait for the right timing and not assert their personal desires or assumptions about what the school needed. As Eloise shared about the Musembe school with friends and family in the States, she continued to garner interest and support for her work in Kenya, especially the possibilities at Musembe.

Only a few months after Eloise returned to the States from her sabbatical in Kenya, an opportunity came her way to raise funds for the Musembe school. Eloise's church family believed in the work she was doing in Kenya, and during the Easter season raised funds for a local and global mission-related project. Although Eloise was not quite sure at the time of how she would direct the funds, her first thought was for clean water, which she knew was a viable need at the school. The share for Musembe from the Easter offering was almost $1,000. Eloise had no idea what would or could be done with the funds, but she and John were committed to partnering with the school to determine a worthwhile project.

Now that Eloise and John had the responsibility to disburse the funds and honor the donors' generosity, Eloise and John needed to develop a plan; more specifically, a strategy they could implement using the principles of cultural humility. The school had not yet articulated their needs or even indicated they wanted to partner with John and Eloise. They first discussed and agreed on several key principles, which were based on their prior experiences with mission and non-profit work and would specifically align with the principles of cultural humility:

1. Any project the school decided to pursue must first benefit the children. The first priority was to the children of the school and to assist with improving the learning conditions.

2. The project must meet the parameters of the available funds. The project could not be so large that it could not be completed. The final goal was a finished project. The added rationale for this stipulation was that Eloise and John also wanted to gauge the commitment and responsibility of the school leaders. Could they use the funds wisely and follow the project to completion in good time? These two factors would then determine whether Eloise and John believed they could move forward with additional projects and develop a collaborative partnership with the Musembe school.

3. Eloise and John did not want to create dependency within the school or community. According to the principles of cultural humility, any project needed to be a true collaborative initiative, with the school and community participating as they were able, and not relying solely on Western money. In no way did Eloise and John want to *do for them*.

4. Accountability for the funds was a priority. Eloise and John wanted to be sure the funds were disbursed in such a way that it would limit temptations for people to help themselves to the money. Having a clear procedure for accountability of the funds would help to deter any attempts for misuse of the funds, and Eloise and John believed this was a practical policy no matter where in the world they were doing mission work.

Eloise's next scheduled visit to Kenya was a few months after her church had raised the funds for the school. Rose arranged for herself and Eloise to attend a meeting at the school. This time, the newly appointed head teacher (principal), Joel, greeted them. As Eloise and Rose sat with the teachers, the atmosphere was greatly different than their first few visits. The school leadership greeted Eloise and Rose warmly and were excited to see Eloise again and by this time fully recognized her! One of the purposes of this visit was to provide this new head teacher with the history of what had transpired with the school to date, with the hope that plans could be made to move forward and continue the work at the school. It was critical to future collaborative work that Joel become acquainted personally with Eloise, Rose, and John in order to understand what efforts had occurred up to this point. It was during this visit that Eloise shared she had brought funds with her for a project. As she told the teachers how much money was available, she laid out the specific guidelines for a project as she and John had discussed and agreed.

The teachers carefully listened as Eloise and Rose outlined the main principles: any project must first benefit the children, and the project must be finished with the available funds. Once those guidelines were stated and agreed to by the entire group, all present in the meeting entered into a discussion about how to proceed with a project. The teachers first deferred to Eloise a number of times and asked what she thought they needed. Eloise continued to tell them she really did not know for certain and wanted them to decide together on a worthwhile project. After some time passed, the new head teacher suggested that he needed a new administration block. The school definitely needed such a building for administrative purposes, but needless to say, this suggestion did not go over well with Eloise at all! She recalls she managed to maintain her professional composure as she firmly reminded this school leader the guiding principles would be that the project must first benefit the children, while an administration block would only benefit him. Eloise could tell by the look on the teachers' faces they clearly understood and supported what she had just said. Finally, one of the female teachers sitting in the back of the room quietly stated, "The children don't have latrines." Eloise was so much in shock at that statement it must have seemed she did not speak for a long time. That statement alone revealed the level of poverty at the school, and Eloise immediately recognized all she did not know about the school and surrounding environment. After a period of silence, Eloise finally replied, "The children will get latrines!"

Everyone responded with applause of great appreciation and gratitude. Eloise also clarified that they thought the school could complete the latrine project with the designated funds. After the school leaders assured Eloise the project was possible with the designated funds, she gave them the permission to move forward as soon as possible. The school leaders created a budget, which John and several other community leaders first vetted then approved, and the funds were gradually released in stages with proper accounting for each phase.

Less than a year later, the latrines had been built just at the edge of the school property; two sets of latrines with four stalls each. The boys had one building and the girls the other. The design included deep enough holes to last for a long time, as well as constructing them well beyond the area which was prone to flooding. Parents from the school had assisted in the building project, thus making it a combined school and community effort. The school leaders had accepted their responsibility and accounted for the funds spent, and also followed up on the progress so that the project would not delay.

The next time Eloise came to Kenya for a visit, the latrines were finished. The school and community leaders proudly showed Eloise and her accompanying education team the completed structures. The school's parent teacher association (PTA) even held a special meeting so they could meet Eloise and her team and thank them in person for the special gift to the entire community. This particular meeting became a special example that Eloise continues to reflect on and share about with others. The community members held their PTA meeting in the morning, and then waited the remainder of the day under the trees until Eloise and her team arrived. As she later learned, these parents were so grateful for the latrines they wanted to thank Eloise in person no matter how long they had to wait for her to arrive. This *attitude of gratitude* was so profound and continues as an example of how even the poorest of the poor were grateful for a basic need.

The latrines were finished. Eloise and John waited again for God to show them what project would be next and how to proceed.

New Classrooms

Another need immediately emerged as the next priority for the school: new classrooms. The structures that constituted the school itself consisted of two permanent classrooms, and four mud rooms which were used for classrooms. The older students utilized the permanent classrooms, which had doors, windows, cement floors, and tin roofs. The younger students used the mud rooms which had open slots for windows, entryways without doors, mud walls, and mud floors. During the rainy season the rain would often come in through the window and door openings, and water would seep in through the floor. The mud rooms, already dark and dreary even in dry season, become more damp and dreary in the rainy season, and ultimately unsuitable for any kind of habitation, especially for students trying to learn and teachers trying to teach. Eloise found out during one of her visits that teachers often sent the younger students home early in advance of an approaching storm. In this way, the students could get home before the torrential rains and wind would hit, and they would not have to endure the horrible conditions in the mud rooms. As Eloise continued to reflect on this situation, she realized that even though the teachers were ultimately concerned for the students' health and well-being, the students were also missing critical learning time. This lack of consistent teaching and learning time during the rainy season was already evident in the students' test scores for each subject. This barrier to the students' education was something to carefully consider as to what could be done.

As Eloise continued to meet with the school leaders to discuss future projects, it was evident that their entire demeanor, outlook, and interactions had changed for the positive since the very first visit. At each visit Eloise asked the question, "What do you need?" She was thinking perhaps they might suggest a well or rainwater tank since the school did not have water on site. But the school leadership had other ideas. This time they requested a new classroom. They presented the rationale that adding a classroom would remove the strain of the existing buildings with the current student population. In addition, other classes could then use the permanent structures so that all could benefit from a healthier learning environment. A new classroom became the next project! This was a good reminder that while working in cross-collaborative efforts of any kind, all involved must keep any assumptions in check and allow the people one is working with to articulate what they need. After all, they do live there and their priorities most likely would not be the priorities of those from the outside.

Eloise went back to the States to raise funds for the new classroom, while John and Rose continued to shepherd the relational efforts in the community. Their role in building and nurturing relationships was crucial to the work God was doing in the community. In addition, the community was beginning to notice what was happening at the school and started to provide support on their own. As plans were made to build the new classroom, the community initiated plans to dig a borehole (well) on site. Their reasoning? If a classroom was going to be built, then water for the project should be on site so that the water did not have to be carried in from long distances. The parents provided the funds and the well was dug. Not only was the water used for the classroom project, it was also filtered with large donated water filters and then used for handwashing and cooking at the school.

When Eloise returned to the village some months later with another team, she was shocked to not only see the well, but the water filters and a feeding program in place for the younger students. When she inquired as to what was going on, the deputy head teacher explained, "The parents are now happy, and they have responded to the needs. They have seen that when even small amounts of funds are combined, much can be accomplished with those funds!"

Young Friends Women's Group

As Eloise was still in the beginning stages of relationship building with the Musembe school during her sabbatical time, another opportunity within the village unexpectedly presented itself to her. John's wife, Rose, and selected other women in the community had formed a women's group in order to support one another in business ventures, social interaction, and spiritual guidance and support. By the time Eloise discovered their work, this group of women already had registered with the county government, had set up bylaws and procedures, and had established a bank account. Many of the women in this original group of sixteen were barely able to support their families, and any extra income would assist with basic needs for their families, as well as providing school fees. This was just the type of venture Eloise had a passion for: support and education for women and girls. However, this time John was not involved. Eloise's new partner was Rose, and John remained in the background in order to allow the women to develop this new venture without his interference. In this way, he demonstrated he was fully supportive of the women's efforts and would only be available to consult as needed.

The women's group was still in its infancy and open to Eloise's guidance. She was not sure how to proceed, but relationship building was of the utmost importance and she knew this process would provide additional information about these women and their group. As Eloise stayed with John and Rose during her sabbatical, she had the opportunity to interact with many of the women from this group. Some had been hired to assist with the maize harvest on the Muhanji farm. Eloise was eager to observe the entire harvest process, especially since it was all manual labor and with different processes than in the U.S. The women showed Eloise how to shuck the maize, and were most delighted when she demonstrated her ability. However, she finally did reveal to them that she had some experience, since she spent time as a young girl on her grandmother's farm in Minnesota and helped there with the corn harvest. As Eloise sat on the floor of the garage with several women, they showed her how to remove the kernels with her thumbs, then how to sort the kernels into the piles for human consumption, and the piles for the animals. They also took time to teach Eloise some basic Swahili words and were delighted when she correctly learned the proper pronunciations and context of their use. It was within these direct interactions that she not only learned the manual tasks of preparing the maize for the next year, but also learned about the personal lives of these women in the community.

As Eloise continued her interactions with the women, she was praying and discerning what the next steps might be for this group. She also had time to reflect on her personal abundance in comparison with the little material resources of these women. Eloise also knew that material resources did not equate to wealth, but that the basic needs of life were critical for each person—access to clean water, access to clean sanitation, safe housing, and food security. Article 25 from the Universal Declaration of Human Rights states:

1. Everyone has the right to a standard of living adequate for the health and well-being of himself and of his family, including food, clothing, housing and medical care and necessary social services, and the right to security in the event of unemployment, sickness, disability, widowhood, old age or other lack of livelihood in circumstances beyond his control.

2. Motherhood and childhood are entitled to special care and assistance. All children, whether born in or out of wedlock, shall enjoy the same social protection.[2]

2. United Nations, *Articles* 1–2.

One day Eloise had clarity in what God was asking her to do. Before Eloise left for Kenya on her sabbatical trip, several friends sent funds along with her for the expressed purpose Eloise use those funds as she would deem appropriate. She had held on to those funds for weeks, waiting and watching for the right opportunity. Those funds were still available. Eloise felt led to use those funds as a seed project for the women's group. They were eager to begin a joint business venture, but needed funding to jump-start their efforts. The funds Eloise had would be the catalyst for the projects of these women, and the completion of this small initiative would let Eloise know if these women would be able to handle larger projects. This women's group was still rather new, and they needed to acquire the skills of working with one another, meeting set deadlines for the work, and each taking responsibility for their share of the work. This beginning project was really a test for them.

The women created a business plan and shared it with Eloise. They kept her updated on their progress, as well as their financial records. This small project was successful, and each woman had an equal percentage of the $100 profit. Although a small amount by American standards, these women were excited about the ability to use these funds to help with various expenses within their families. More importantly, these women now recognized the potential of this group and gained in their own self-confidence as entrepreneurs.

Throughout the next year, this women's group was awarded several grants which they used to increase their business ventures. Each woman either began a new business or expanded an existing one. In addition, they divided themselves into smaller groups and each of those groups jointly entered into another business venture. In this way, all of the women benefited together, and each received a share of the dividends from the group businesses at the end of the year.

As the women gained confidence in their business efforts, another interesting phenomenon was taking place, in that they were recognizing the need to become leaders within the community and take on various social justice efforts which would benefit the community. Eloise taught sessions on servant leadership along with other leadership concepts to these women when she visited the village. The practical application of those concepts was bearing fruit in practice as they became vital partners in new initiatives within the community.

The village and the surrounding area was in need of such an example as these women were providing. In Kenyan culture, it is not common for people to volunteer their time for a cause or a social effort. Often there is expectation of some sort of compensation. For these women, they were living out and modeling the biblical mandate to meet the needs of the poor, needy, orphaned, and widowed.

Sanitary Supplies for School Girls

As Eloise continued her work in Kenya with John, she had the opportunity to visit many Quaker secondary schools. As Eloise asked about the challenges these schools faced, one main theme kept rising to the surface: girls often missed school during their monthly periods because they did not have sanitary supplies. As a result, for approximately one week every month, girls would stay home during their periods and miss school. As they missed their coursework and studies, they would then fall behind academically. In addition, if girls were home during the day, they would often become victims of men in the community looking for easy sexual targets. Overall, not only it is safer for girls to be in school during the day, but the academic focus is critical to their development and their future. For the majority of girls in developing countries and in impoverished regions around the world, girls are mostly marginalized and are the least educated, have little to no economic freedom, have limited opportunities to earn an income from respectable sources, and are often isolated within the community.[3] Further, for girls in these same backgrounds, the onset of menstruation is still treated according to traditional culture as the indicator that a girl is now ready to become sexually active and get married, and therefore school is no longer a priority or even important.[4] Here then, was an opportunity to discover just what was needed for the girls from Musembe and if the community would support any assistance for these girls. Early adolescence provides a critical window of opportunity to intervene at a time when girls are experiencing many challenges, but before those challenges have resulted in outcomes which may be irreversible. A lack of economic assets has also been cited as a barrier to translating sexual and reproductive health knowledge into behavior change, especially during adolescence, as

3. Kenya Demographic and Health Survey, *The DHS Program*, 23–43.
4. Lloyd, *New Lessons*, 27.

girls are often financially dependent on men and therefore lose decision-making power in their sexual relationships.[5]

At one of the secondary schools Eloise visited during one of her trips, Levi, the principal, shared his story of how he learned about this very issue the girls faced at his school. He observed that some of the girls would walk around school with their sweaters tied around their waists and he would chastise them for not properly wearing their school uniforms. The girls would ashamedly comply with his direction to put their sweaters on properly. One day, one of the female teachers at the school took Levi aside and shared the reason the girls were wearing their sweaters around their waists and why their attendance was often sporadic. She explained the girls did not have sanitary supplies and were embarrassed during their monthly periods. Levi was immediately ashamed of his attitude and lack of knowledge of the girls' issues. After all, he was a father of girls himself, but he did not even make the connection with the girls in his school. Levi immediately took action and gathered sanitary supplies to keep on hand at the school. In addition, he applied for a grant from an NGO which would provide continuous supplies for the girls at his school. Not only did the attendance of the girls at his school improve, their academic performance followed suit. This new knowledge planted a seed in the back of Eloise's mind which would become useful later on.

As Eloise continued her work with the Musembe school, the story of Levi's school and the issue of sanitary supplies kept coming to her mind. She finally asked Rose if there was a similar problem at Musembe. Rose consulted with the female teachers at Musembe and they confirmed the girls often missed school because of lack of sanitary supplies. In addition, the academic performance of the girls was also low as a result of missing class days. Here was another opportunity to assist the girls from this school and village. The next step was to discern what could be done to support the girls of Musembe.

Eloise went home once again and shared her concerns about the girls and lack of sanitary supplies with her friends and supporters. However, this time she faced some interesting challenges of others involved in such global efforts. One group of women in Eloise's area had been sewing reusable cloth sanitary napkins to send overseas to Uganda and India. They suggested Eloise arrange for this type of approach for the girls at Musembe. The rationale was that supplies could be purchased locally in the village,

5. Kenya Demographic and Health Survey, *The DHS Program*, 23–53.

and then women could be employed there to make the supplies for the girls. Eloise thought the idea sounded like a very practical solution and began to take the steps to move forward with that plan. However, before any commitments were made to the project, Eloise consulted her friend Rose for advice and presented her with the two options, paper sanitary supplies or the reusable cloth ones. Rose replied back to Eloise's inquiry that cloth napkins would not be a solution for their region. Rose stated they had deep pit latrines, and paper products could be easily disposed of in those latrines. In addition, Rose brought up another important point. Washing the cloth supplies would be less sanitary all around because of the lack of water supplies in their area. Most homes in the Musembe region have to haul water from the river to the home, which is already burdensome for the families. Issues with lack of access to clean water and water-related diseases are common in this area, making paper products the most viable solution for these girls. This example was a great reminder for Eloise that although the cloth supplies might be a practical solution for some places around the world, it was not a practical solution for Musembe and Muliro Village. This region had different needs. The women had spoken.

As the sanitary supplies project for the Musembe girls gained momentum, Eloise continued her conversations with Rose to organize this new project and together they outlined the details of the implementation. The women's group took the lead to purchase the supplies locally at the retail rates to benefit local shopkeepers, organize the supplies into packages for each girl, then deliver the supplies to the school. The women's group collaborated with the school leaders to design a special program to carry out this project. In concert with the women teachers, the women's group arranged for a class session with the class (grade) 8 girls to not only teach them the proper use of the supplies, but also instruct them in basic life skills. The first session was a rousing success, with the girls and their families expressing gratitude for these basic supplies. Through this effort, the women also became the mentors and role models for these girls, who had few such positive role models in their lives. The women in turn recognized that their efforts were a critical component to the development of these girls not only at Musembe, but for their futures, and ultimately the future of the entire village.

When Eloise later returned to the Musembe school with a group of educators for professional development workshops with the teachers, one of their scheduled events was to collaborate with the female teachers and the women's group to provide a health and counseling session for that year's class 8 girls and then give them their supplies of pads and panties. As was the custom after a special session or event, the girls were asked to give a *vote of thanks*. The girls' leader for the school carried out her duty as a leader and expressed her gratitude on behalf of all the girls for their gifts. She also reminded the others that of all the areas in the world professor Eloise and her team could have gone, God directed them to Musembe of all places, and they should all be grateful. This young girl further stated that she had only seen White people before from a distance, but through the interactions between Eloise, her team, and the girls, this girl now knew these Americans were real people just like she and her classmates were.

The words the adolescent girl spoke that day became a deep cultural lesson for Eloise and her entire team. These girls also had biases and assumptions of *mzungus*, White people. However, as those girls interacted with Eloise and her team during their time in the village, those biases and assumptions changed. All the interactions as a part of this sanitary supply project were vital for both groups in their understanding of the other. One of Eloise's team members shared later in a group debrief session about the girls' responses to the sanitary supplies, "I was filled with so much emotion because of how they were receiving the gifts. It was . . . I mean, the things we gave them—they're necessities. We did not give each of them a car or TV; we gave them necessities. And they were so appreciative."

This discussion of basic needs and gratitude continued on through the remaining time this team was in Kenya. Their observations noted that people did not have many things in their lives which provide distractions in the way Americans have. The cultural lesson for this group was that material things were not important. The basic needs of life and family were priorities for the Kenyans in this village, and this lesson impacted Eloise and her team.

During one of Eloise's follow-up visits to Musembe, she gained permission to personally interview a sampling of the class 8 girls about their life challenges. The girls she interviewed came from the local slum area and are considered the poorest of the poor at Musembe. When asked about their access to the sanitary supplies, all of the girls stated that they did not have the funds for supplies during their monthly periods, so they had to stay home from school, but would prefer to be in school. One girl said she would come to school no matter what since she did not want to remain home at all. Some girls tried to beg supplies from female friends and relatives, but the majority just were not able to find the supplies they needed. They all said that they were grateful for the program of the women's group in providing the sanitary supplies. This theme of gratefulness was still present even several years later in these girls' responses.

As this program for sanitary supplies continued, it also became necessary to evaluate the processes and procedures of the program, as well as determining if the program should continue. Three years after Eloise and Rose's group began this initiative, Eloise examined the school data for attendance and academic records of the girls. In addition, she interviewed both male and female teachers regarding attitudes and dispositions of the girls. What the data showed was very encouraging. First, the attendance for the girls receiving the supplies increased, but so did the attendance for all of the girls. Secondly, the girls now in class 8 were making noticeable gains academically, and some were now on par with some of the boys. In addition, girls in the lower grades were making gains—girls who had not yet been a part of the sanitary supply program. The overall effort in mentoring girls in life skills was spilling over into the younger classes. Finally, when Eloise collected this round of data, there were no pregnancies reported within class 8 as in previous years. When Eloise asked the teachers why, the teachers responded that the girls now had more self-worth than before and attributed this self-worth to the sanitary supply program and the mentoring of Rose and her women's group. God's work was evident in this community as the results showed. The program had to continue.

Feeding Program

Each time Eloise was in Kenya even from the start of her work there, it seemed God had a specific lesson for her to learn. The topic of hunger was another such lesson. Eloise was a continuous learner of everything and anything related to Kenya and Africa. In preparation for one of her trips she had been reading a book which described the issues of hunger throughout the country, and specifically how hunger affects children in their learning. She was not quite sure what to do with that information, except to keep her eyes and ears open to learn what she could while in the country. One important aspect of Eloise's learning was to visit schools as often as she could. As an educator, she continues to be a life-long learner, and school visits helped to build relationships with principals and teachers while learning more about the Kenyan educational system. As she visits mostly

Quaker schools throughout western Kenya, she usually begins with one of her common questions: "What challenges do you face in your school?" This one open-ended question allows for many types of responses, which then leads to follow-up questions for more in-depth learning. During this particular visit to Kenya, every school reported that the topic of hunger was a major challenge. Especially during the times of year before the maize harvest, children were often limited to one meal a day, or sometimes less than that. Some of the schools had initiated lunch programs, which ensured the children would receive at least one substantial meal a day while school was in session.

It was while visiting one of the day schools Eloise once again came face to face with an issue of extreme hunger. While touring the school grounds with one of her Kenyan colleagues, the principal took them to inspect the dining hall. As they were standing outside of the dining hall, Eloise noticed two young boys with a plate and a spoon walking along the outside wall of the dining hall and peering into the windows. As she continued to observe these boys, the principal also took notice and commented that the boys must be hungry. She called the boys over to her and they came to her as frightened animals. As the principal talked with the boys, she confirmed to Eloise and her colleague that these boys were in the stages of starvation and pointed out the specific physical signs of starvation. The principal then called out to one of her high school students to come and take the boys to the kitchen so they could get some food. Eloise's heart became heavy from this experience and she turned aside to gather her composure before she could continue the tour of the school property. The thought kept running through her mind: "What about the students of Musembe? Are they hungry?"

When Eloise saw John a few days later after the observation of hunger at that school, she asked him about the students of Musembe. He confirmed they were also hungry, especially in the months before the next harvest, known as the hunger season. Eloise had already been thinking about what could be done at Musembe and her first response to John was, "We need to start a feeding program for Musembe!" John did not disagree with Eloise's concern or her idea, but he also wanted to discuss a solution which would be realistic and manageable. Eloise had been thinking big, but John was wise in his response to discuss all of the implications of such a program and what would be manageable. For example, if they started a program to feed the entire school, the financial commitment could become too much for them and their supporters to maintain. Further, if they started a feeding program, the result could draw other students to the school, which would then put a strain on the school's overextended facilities and resources. After much prayer and discussion, John and Eloise decided they should begin small and start with a feeding program for the class 8 candidates during their week of national exams. In that way, Eloise and John could begin such a project and keep it manageable, while still providing the Musembe students the necessary nourishment during that critical time at the conclusion of their primary education.

As Eloise and John finalized their idea for the feeding program in consultation with the school leadership, the women's group also became a crucial partner to carry out this project. The women eagerly accepted the challenge and engaged in the planning. However, they took it one step further. Not only did the women plan for lunch for the class 8 students, but they included breakfast, morning devotions, and a snack at the end of the day. Even during that first effort, the government testing officials who were monitoring the exams remarked they were impressed with the positive environment at the school, and they had not seen anything like it before. God was already blessing this new initiative.

Scholarships for the Students

As fund-raising efforts continued for the needs in the village, Eloise and John continued to discern next steps for the Musembe school. Ongoing conversations with the teachers and community members were a vital source of information. Through some of those conversations, John discovered that when students completed class 8 at Musembe, it was the end of their formal schooling. In the Kenyan school system, if a child does not earn high enough scores to be accepted to high school, their class 8 education is the end of their school career. The majority of the students do not have the monetary resources to even attend a trade school or other training after class 8, thus limiting their future work to mostly menial labor. As John learned about these issues, he shared with Eloise these concerns and they began to consider a way forward to help students go to high school. They began to brainstorm: What about offering scholarships to high school for students from Musembe?

Background knowledge about barriers to education was also important in assessing this need for further education for Musembe students, and how additional education could benefit students and the community for the long term. For example, according to research from Dawo and Simatwa, the rate of primary school completion in Kenya was 82 percent from 2000 to 2006, with only 68 percent completion for girls.[6] Data from the Kenyan Bureau of Statistics also showed that more girls started primary school than boys, but dropped out in more numbers by the time they would have finished primary school.[7]

According to household survey data provided by Unicef in their 2015 report on *Findings from the Global Initiative on Out-of-School Children*, the countries of Ethiopia, Kenya, Somalia, and the United Republic of Tanzania accounted for almost one half of children not attending school in all of Eastern and Southern Africa.[8] Primary education is a critical component for foundational development of a child, but secondary education provides additional life skills necessary for increasing economic capacity for the rest of a child's life.[9] In addition, more education benefits women economically and is shown to positively influence main health-related issues such as: proper nutrition, pre-natal health care, infant and mortality rates, and the reduction of early pregnancy rates.[10]

As Eloise and John discussed the need of high school scholarships for Musembe students, Eloise was at first only interested in offering scholarships to girls, for a number of specific reasons. First, girls are still marginalized members of society in Kenya, especially in the rural communities. Traditional gender roles generally favor boys for education while girls are considered a labor commodity, which then competes with their education. Even if girls are allowed to go to school, for the most part they are still required to help at home with various chores, thus limiting their ability to focus on their studies.[11] Boys are given preference for education since the belief is that girls will only be wives and mother and do not need any education beyond the primary grades. Extreme poverty also limits access to education, especially for girls.[12] While Eloise had data to back up her assumptions and beliefs, John reminded her that equity was also important

6. Dawo and Simatwa, Opportunities and Challenges, 730–741.

7. Kenya Demographic and Health Survey, *The DHS Program*, 23–43.

8. UNESCO Institute for Statistics, *Fixing the Broken Promise*, 5–10.

9. Ibid., 5–10.

10. Ibid., 5–10.

11. Ibid., 5–10.

12. Ibid., 510.

in any work they would undertake. While it would be noble to focus on the girls' education, the boys should not be left behind. In fact, since Kenya has begun a major focus on *girl child education*, the pendulum has swung the other way and boys have been left behind in the educational process and almost ignored. After much discussion and prayer once again, Eloise and John agreed that scholarships would be provided to both girls and boys.

Fund-raising in the U.S. for the projects in Kenya were going well, but how would Eloise and John begin this effort and sustain it? They first had to agree on the criteria for selection for a scholarship to high school. If based on need alone, all of the students were needy. In fact, most of them were from the local sum area and the families had little to no extra resources for basic needs, let alone for expenses such as high school tuition and fees. Eloise and John finally decided their beginning point: offering a scholarship to the top-performing girl and boy on the national test taken at the end of class 8. As word spread throughout the community about this potential opportunity, excitement mounted as the test results were announced. However, Eloise and John had a little bit of a miscommunication they first needed to resolve.

When Eloise was checking on the funding available for scholarships for high school, she knew the Africa fund account had enough money to fully fund one student for high school for four years. Eloise and John had set the goal at four years so that they would be sure the child could stay in school all four years and not have to worry if enough funds were available or not. Eloise desired to be a good steward of the funds people had donated for the Kenya projects, so she told John they could fund one student—or so she thought. Even though she and John had discussed the scholarship plan over the phone, it was a text message exchange which caused a mix-up. John thought Eloise had said to go ahead and fund a girl and a boy, so John communicated that information to the school. When the national test scores were released, Eloise reported there were only funds for one scholarship, so she wanted to select the girl who had qualified. As she faced an assembly of students at Musembe, she announced the scholarship for the top girl, Mildred. It was then Eloise learned of the mix-up in communication. The boy who had the top score was at the assembly and had believed he would receive a scholarship because of his scores and what had been communicated to the community. The boy ran home in tears and became depressed, refusing to even eat for several days. When Eloise heard about the boy's emotional state she was obviously devastated about the mix-up but

99

was unsure how to proceed. She consulted with John and Rose and tried to determine what could be done. As she prayed about the issue, she sent an email home to her supporters sharing the mix-up and her concern for this boy who was so devastated he would not be able to go to high school after all. By God's grace, when Eloise woke up the next morning and checked her email, one of her prayer partners responded they would sponsor young Daniel for the four years of high school! Through the miscommunication, God provided a solution for future scholarships Eloise and John had not even considered yet—that of sponsorships for the students. Mildred and Daniel became the first students ever from Musembe to attend high school, which resulted in rejoicing throughout the community. Their students now had a chance for continued education and a better future for themselves and their families.

Through this example of the scholarships, Eloise and John learned a valuable lesson about the importance of clear and explicit communication. They also knew they needed to accept responsibility for their role in the mix-up and not blame the other. The way they handled even minor conflict with one another needed to be within the realm of cultural humility and respect for the other. Even though they had discussed the scholarship process, the communication had not been clear. Effective communication can be a major challenge in cross-cultural work, especially when one culture is more direct in communication than the other. Once the scholarship issue had been resolved and Daniel was on his way to high school, John showed Eloise their text message exchange. When Eloise saw the words she had written, she knew they were open to a different interpretation than what she had intended. Eloise readily admitted her mistake and apologized to John. Even more importantly, John never once said to Eloise, "I told you so." Eloise and John moved forward from that point with the resolve to improve their communication with each other. Mistakes and misunderstandings will happen, but how we handle those mistakes is critical to building effective working relationships within the framework of cultural humility.

Professional Development Workshops

As relationship building continued with the school and community, the school leaders asked if Eloise could bring teachers with her on one of her trips to deliver professional development workshop sessions. Without giving a firm promise, she assured them she would take their request under consideration. In this way, if she could not find a team of teachers to join her, then she was not breaking a promise. In the Kenyan culture, even saying "I will see what I can do" could be interpreted as a promise. Eloise and the teachers also discussed some potential topics which could be included in a two-day workshop session. As they articulated their needs, Eloise realized again she did not have all of the necessary background information. She did not understand the children they were working with, or the limitations in resources or teacher preparation. However, she was prepared to learn all she could in preparation for this next project. At times the challenges of the extreme needs in the village seemed to be overwhelming, but John continued to remind Eloise they needed to begin small and keep things manageable. That continues to be wise advice.

Less than two years after Eloise and John's first visit to the Musembe school, Eloise brought along of team of four educators from the U.S. to conduct the first professional development session at Musembe. With Rose's guidance, another neighboring primary school was invited so they could also benefit from the U.S team's visit.

This first professional development team involved people other than George Fox faculty colleagues. Through Eloise's work at the university, her graduate students and others in the community had caught the vision of the work she and John were doing in rural Kenya and wanted to participate. Inviting others into the vision and work in Muliro Village was an exciting opportunity. However, with the opportunity came immense responsibilities. Not only was Eloise responsible for the group as team leader, but she felt the weight of preparing this first group for the professional development teaching sessions, in addition to the cultural preparations.

Eloise and John discussed the type of Kenyan cultural knowledge which would be an integral component for the group preparation. It was important to prepare for the culture aspects, but not to over-prepare. Learning about basic cultural expectations and norms is one thing, but experiencing those first hand is something a person cannot adequately prepare for ahead of time. Eloise selected several key resources to assist the group with the cultural information she believed would address Kenyan culture in general, but also contain principles of cultural humility, which was the overarching philosophy for the entire trip and the preparations. Each participant was required to read selections from the following resources:

- *The Last Hunger Season: A Year in an African Farm Community on the Brink of Change* (Roger Thurow, 2012)

- *Cross-Cultural Servanthood: Serving the World in Christlike Humility,* (Duane Elmer, 2006)

- "Cultural Humility: A Framework for Local and Global Engagement" (Eloise Hockett, Linda Samek, and Scot Headley, 2013)

The pre-trip planning sessions included preparations for the content Eloise and her team would be sharing with the teachers in attendance. The teachers prioritized a list of topics they believed would further assist with their work in their classrooms.

Eloise and her group first created a basic schedule for their teaching days. Since she had already presented numerous workshops in Kenya, she was familiar with the overall structure, as well as cultural expectations for the day. Rose also assisted in the pre-workshop planning by meeting with the school leaders, then sending emails to Eloise for clarifications. This partnership was invaluable, in that she had a reliable partner on site in Kenya working with her in all of the preparations.

The daily structure included time for opening introductory remarks at the start of each day, tea breaks, lunch, and end-of-the-day group debriefing sessions. As Eloise and her group developed the overall schedule, the structure was set so that Eloise, as team leader, would teach the first introductory sessions, then allow the other team members to team teach and plan the remaining sessions. While one person was teaching, the rest of the team would interact and participate right along with the Kenyan teachers and leaders. The rationale for this strategy was to help the team members acclimate to the type of teaching, pacing, and interactions which would be culturally appropriate, in addition to integrating with the Kenyan teachers. At one point during the planning sessions, one of the team members suggested, "Let's just take out the opening part so that we have more time for our teaching." This statement provided a key opportunity for Eloise to explain the importance of the Kenyans' cultural practice of welcoming visitors, introducing the event and setting the stage for the work to come. It was also important for the team to be reminded they were guests in another culture and needed to be respectful to the Kenyans' practices and procedures and not assert their own agenda.[13] This attitude demonstrated humility in practice and served as the foundation for the work in the village.

Once Eloise and her team arrived in the village, the learning curve was high for the rest of the team. This team of U.S. teachers were committed to

---

13. Elmer, *Cross-cultural Servanthood*, 140.

the trip and dedicated to teach the content they had prepared. But more importantly, they were also committed to learning as much about the culture as possible. In order to engage with the culture at a deeper level, Eloise arranged for this team to stay in homes and not in a local guesthouse or hotel. Throughout their time with their Kenyan hosts and the teachers in Muliro Village, all began forming strong bonds with one another. Conversations and interactions occurred before sessions, during breaks, during meals, after the sessions concluded for the day, and well into the night in the homes. The U.S. team also participated in group sessions with the Kenyan teachers while another member was teaching. Interacting with each other was the primary focus. The Kenyan teachers also became teachers to Eloise's team in sharing cultural songs and dances, basic Swahili words, and giving each person a Kenyan name to commemorate the event. These types of authentic interactions do not just happen without intentional and ongoing relationship building.

This first professional development session was a learning experience for all involved. First of all, Eloise's group had been invited for this initial professional development session. As the relationships continued to build between Eloise, John, and Rose, the teachers trusted all of them to assist in areas where the school had need. The teachers acknowledged both their needs and desires for more training in teaching pedagogy in order to help their students. Eloise and her team were able to provide the content these teachers needed in order to better serve the students in the Musembe school and the surrounding village. These efforts were bearing fruit, and all believed there was more to come. Once again, Eloise and John would wait and see what doors God would open next.

7

New Initiatives and Possibilities

As the work at Musembe Primary School and Muliro Village continued to develop and make progress, Eloise and John were continually contacted by friends in the U.S. and elsewhere with inquiries of ways to assist various groups and communities in Kenya. Even though most all of the requests appeared to be worthy of consideration, each one needed to be carefully evaluated in order to discern if the project would fit within the scope of the work Eloise and John were already doing in Kenya, and if those requests would align with Eloise and John's philosophical and service beliefs utilizing the guiding principles of cultural humility. Even more importantly, Eloise and John needed to carefully consider the various steps in their planning process so that any new project or involvement with outside groups would be truly collaborative and not lead to dependency on those they would be assisting. This philosophy was always one of their primary objectives.

Engaging others from the U.S. and other countries in Kenya through service and mission work remains a high priority for Eloise and John. Through John's connections with his work at Friends United Meeting, many people have caught the vision of the Quaker work in Kenya and have not only been interested in various projects, but have also desired to actively participate in the projects alongside the Kenyans. The same also holds true for Eloise and her connections at George Fox and throughout her church community. Eloise and John believe wonderful opportunities abound for expanding participation in their various projects, in addition to beginning new ones. However, they also realize the immense responsibility of providing authentic experiences which utilize the skills and abilities of those participating in a service-learning or mission trip.

One recent example of a possible new initiative illustrates how not all collaborative efforts will pan out as intended. Another non-profit organization in the States contacted Eloise and John about possibly partnering with them primarily because of their experience with collaborative initiatives in Kenya. Eloise and John were excited about this potential opportunity to further serve the Quaker church in Kenya via another approach which would involve children. They took time one afternoon to meet with the group's point person Cindy (name changed), in order to discuss various options for collaborating on a new initiative focused on youth in Kenya. After several hours of discussion, the meeting ended with all of them agreeing on a plan of next steps and a draft timeline of when and how to begin this new work with youth in Kenya. After some months passed, Eloise heard via another source that Cindy had decided to divert from the plan she had created with Eloise and John to an alternate plan for the next steps, but had not informed them. Cindy finally came to meet with Eloise for advice on how to proceed with her alternate plan. Since she came specifically to seek advice, Eloise asked specific questions for clarifications, then made suggestions she believed could be helpful for Cindy as she proceeded with her project in Kenya. Eloise immediately contacted John and they discussed this interaction and the overall situation. Eloise and John finally came to agreement they could not become involved with this organization or Cindy at this time, nor probably even in the future. First, when they had left the initial meeting together, they had all agreed on a plan for collaboration, and Cindy diverted from the plan without the courtesy of notifying Eloise or John. Secondly, Eloise and John wondered if the lack of notification or contact indicated perhaps Cindy could not be trusted to follow through in the initial stages of a project, so how could she be trusted once they were in the middle of a project? Trusted relationships are critical to any kind of collaborative work and even though this initiative fizzled, it was a good reminder to enter into any kind of initiative with a discerning mind, along with a bit of caution, especially in the initial planning stages. Still, Eloise and John are committed to lifelong learning regarding how best to engage in collaborative work with people from all walks of life, whether in Kenya, the U.S., or other places where God calls them to serve.

Nursing Student Initiative

As Eloise continued her work in Kenya and shared those experiences with students and colleagues at George Fox, others soon became interested in those projects and felt a calling to partner with Eloise and John. One of those examples came by way of the nursing program at George Fox. When Eloise took her first group of teachers to Musembe to deliver a professional development workshop to the teachers at the school, a nurse educator was a member of that team. As she saw the health needs of the communities and the deteriorating conditions of one of the rural hospitals, this nurse, along with Eloise and John, began to brainstorm the possibilities of combining health care and education within their existing work in Kenya. After thoroughly discussing various options, they all came to a very practical solution: Why not involve the nursing program at George Fox and integrate the disciplines of nursing and education through a service-learning experience within the framework of cultural humility?

Service-learning, a program already used in many higher education institutions, combines the skills of various content disciplines and then utilizes those skills within specific service projects. The major elements of service-learning include: (a) the components of collaboration with a specific community, (b) bringing theory from the classroom into practice, and (c) providing an opportunity for students to increase their cultural competency.[1] When these definitions are applied together, especially for the university student, service-learning experiences provide a value-added component for the students' overall learning, and often have long-term benefits for the participants and the communities they serve long after the program has been completed.[2] Furthermore, the goals for service-learning can be adaptable to groups outside of the university as well.

Considering the objectives of service-learning and cultural humility, involving the nursing students from George Fox would be a natural connection to the existing work in Kenya. Many nursing programs, including the one at George Fox, have implemented the recommendations from the American Nurses Association and the American Association of Colleges of Nursing (AACN), "Baccalaureate Essentials." Both of these organizations mandate that nurses become equipped to provide quality care coupled with

---

1. Bently and Ellison, Increasing Cultural Competence, 208.
2. Doll et al., Transforming Practice, 175.

appropriate cultural competence and sensitivity.[3] Cultural humility, within the context of service-learning, expands on these cultural competency goals to: build relationships; utilize intentional listening skills; set aside biases and assumptions; and work collaboratively with others in the mindset of co-learning. Taken together, a service-learning trip to Kenya for student nurses could most definitely help meet those cultural competency goals, while at the same time strengthening the students' knowledge and skills of medical care. Further, the nursing students would also encounter diseases not common in the U.S. and observe different methods of delivering medical care, often with limited resources.

As the discussions ensued regarding involving the nursing students and faculty, Eloise and John carefully considered and discussed many factors. To begin with, the medical needs all over Kenya are already overwhelming, especially due to a shortage of qualified doctors and nurses, and medical costs are too high for the majority of the people to pay. According to one of Kenya's young and upcoming doctors, there are eight thousand licensed physicians in Kenya for a population of over forty-six million. However, only about four thousand are currently practicing in the country's public hospitals since the government pay is inadequate. About five hundred physicians work in private hospitals and the rest have left the country for higher-paying jobs elsewhere. Most of the physicians also practice in higher-populated areas. The needs of the rural communities are even more serious, since there are not enough medical facilities in the remote areas to treat the most basic of illnesses, resulting in patients often waiting until it is too late to seek medical care.

One of Eloise's Kenyan friends who grew up near Mt. Elgon further clarified the local perception about health care. In general, Kenyans believe matter-of-factly that death is a part of life. When a person becomes ill, the perception, especially among the uneducated, is that the illness is their appointed time to die. For example, when John's wife, Rose, was diagnosed with cancer a few years ago, most of the people in their community believed it was an automatic death sentence. When she returned to church and community activities six months after her treatments, the people were shocked and at first acted as if they had seen a ghost. Rose has since used her own health experience with cancer to promote health prevention initiatives, especially for women.

---

3. Kohlbry, *Culture: A Critical Review of Concepts*, 304.

Not only were all the needs great in these rural areas, but the local leaders were almost begging Eloise for additional support for health care. If the George Fox nursing program would enter into a partnership with the ongoing initiatives in the rural areas such as Muliro Village and the Kaptama hospital on Mt. Elgon, how would the team approach the medical care so it would not be too overwhelming for one small group, and how would they plan for such an effort to keep it manageable for all involved? These and other questions had to be thoroughly discussed before a new initiative could be planned for and implemented.

As Eloise and John continued to discuss this new possibility with involving nursing students, they agreed as they had with other new initiatives they would need to begin small. Having a smaller project would hopefully keep it manageable and help to ensure the success of that project. In this case, once the first trip with nursing students was completed, Eloise, John, and the nursing faculty involved could then debrief together and assess the entire program from start to finish and make recommendations for the next trip. It was within this context that plans moved forward to bring the first group of nursing students from George Fox University to Kenya to partner with the local people in Muliro Village first, then to Kaptama hospital. Eloise and John had several reasons for deciding on these two projects. First, relationships with key people already existed and were thriving in both of these communities. With the specific initiatives already underway and making progress in Muliro Village, the health care focus would build on these relationships and add a critical component for a holistic effort in the village. An emphasis on health assessments and health care education would round out the efforts on sanitation, clean water, sanitary supplies for the girls, and further education for the students.

For the hospital at Kaptama, the staff especially needed encouragement and support. Kaptama was located in the very region where the Kenyan police set up camp as they were fighting the militia groups on the mountain. Even though several years had passed since the ceasefire and the Kenyan police left, the people within this area had not yet recovered from their trauma, and the hospital had also suffered. Not only were resources scarce, but the buildings needed repair, and one building project which had started before the fighting was still left unfinished. Even though there were government health care facilities just up the road higher on the mountain and a few other clinics down the road toward the lower land, the people would not go to any of them for treatment. As John traveled throughout the region after the war to meet with local leaders and church officials, he would often stop at the hospital and wonder what could be done there and if the place was really making a difference. During one of his visits, he soon discovered why Kaptama was important to this region. A high school–aged girl from the forest region had been brutally raped and was rushed to Kaptama for treatment. Along the way the girl and her family had bypassed a government hospital and several other smaller health centers. As John witnessed the intake of this girl and the staff prepped her for treatment, he became overwhelmed with emotion and excused himself from the scene for a few minutes. It was within those moments of grief for the girl and her condition John knew he must find some way to build up Kaptama's hospital. Had the hospital not been there, the girl would not have been taken anywhere else and only God knows what might have been her fate. As John shared this experience with Eloise, he knew the clinical staff would benefit from additional support on site to assist with an influx of various medical needs, and this collaborative approach would be an important learning experience for the students in learning *from* others. Even more so, John believed this effort would demonstrate to the community there were people in other places of the world who cared deeply for them and desired to assist them via health care support. This effort would then be one more step in bringing healing to this mountain.

Based on discussions with the leaders from Muliro Village and the Kaptama hospital as to what they specifically needed for such an outreach, Eloise and John decided on the following approach for this first service-learning trip for these nursing students. First, the nursing students would provide basic health assessments to the students of the Musembe school. These assessments would provide key insights into the level of health needs for the students and assist the school personnel in understanding how to support students with health issues in their learning. For example, an eye screening would identify students who had vision issues, so the teachers could place those students in the front of the classroom and ensure they could see work on the blackboard and on paper. This type of information for teachers would become a piece of the education focus of the trip. Part two of the health emphasis in the village would entail providing basic health assessments and vision exams to widows of the village. The women's group in Muliro Village would select twenty of the neediest widows in the area and invite them to come for the health assessments. In addition, the widows would be given food supplies to assist with their basic needs. Most of the widows in these rural communities are also victims of extreme food insecurity or poor diets, which in turn affects their health.

For the second part of this initial service-learning trip, the nursing students would observe the clinical staff at the Kaptama hospital and assist with basic patient care as appropriate, with an emphasis on learning from the staff and respectful sharing together as professionals. As the churches were finding new life in the Kaptama region through the discipleship training John was shepherding, and the schools were benefitting from professional development, the lack of quality health care in the area also required consideration. With adding support for health care, the attention was now becoming a holistic approach on the mountain, focusing on spiritual development, education, and health care, all carefully developed with the local community and through the principles of cultural humility.

Eloise and her nursing colleague, Stephanie Fisher, began planning for this new venture at their home base in Oregon, while John continued with the planning in Kenya for this first student nursing team from George Fox. Communication was vital as they tried to anticipate how all of the details for such an initiative would fall into place, what types of supplies might be required at both locations, and how to adequately prepare the students for such an experience. For this first service-learning nursing trip to Kenya, Stephanie stepped in to fill the role of Eloise's former colleague who had been visioning with her about this project and had visited the actual sites in Kenya where they would be working. Even though Stephanie had vital knowledge of nursing practices and cross-cultural experience and had traveled to other developing countries and served in Ghana on a medical mission trip, she had never been to the sites in Kenya where the team was planning to carry out these service-learning projects. Eloise had been to these proposed sites multiple times for education work and had a strong foundation of the cultural aspects, but did not have the medical background to advise in that part of the planning process. However, Eloise, Stephanie, and John believed God was calling them all to collaborate in this venture and viewed it as an incredible opportunity to prepare nursing students cross-culturally outside of a familiar context. What, then, was the best way to prepare these students?

The nursing students selected for this first trip to Kenya had applied for the trip and submitted written essays which addressed specific prompts related to their desire to go on such a trip, their attitudes of cross-cultural interactions, and what they believed they might learn from such an experience. Only senior nursing students were invited to apply, and only five met the criteria of the application process. The students were offered a one-credit elective course related to planning for the trip to Kenya, and the entire team met weekly for eight weeks to prepare as best as possible.

The main topics for the trip preparation included: cultural practices of the region, tropical disease, and general medical knowledge. The professors assigned required readings related to cultural sensitivity and tropical diseases, and Stephanie used her medical expertise to guide the students to recognize the basic symptoms of tropical diseases. Eloise engaged students in discussions of different cultural aspects related to the regions where they would be serving. Even though the rural areas where they would be engaging in service learning and ministry were less than two hours by car, the regions were inhabited by different tribal groups who spoke their own distinctive local languages and whose cultural practices varied from the other. It was imperative to ready the group as best as possible to be mentally, emotionally, and spiritually ready for the cultural differences and interactions with the Kenyans in their homes, in the broader community, as well as in the clinical settings. In addition, it was even more important for all members of the team to realize that the people they interacted with would be carefully observing the Christian witness of this team through their attitudes, words, and actions.

John assisted in the trip preparations via video conferencing as a way to make connections with the entire group before they arrived in Kenya, as well as to help answer questions related to culture and the sites the team would visit. The overall trip preparations were truly a joint effort between the George Fox group in the U.S. and John in Kenya, thus demonstrating the framework of cultural humility through co-learning and collaboration.

This first service-learning trip for the nursing students from George Fox occurred in late March 2015 during the university's spring break. The trip became a pilot trip as Eloise, John, and Stephanie carefully assessed all aspects of the preparation related to culture interactions, medical care, and learning, as well as the final outcomes in order to answer the question: Would they collaborate on such an initiative again? The answer was a resounding yes! All three believed this first collaborative effort in bringing nursing students to Kenya for a service-learning trip was successful in many ways. First, the people in Muliro Village were grateful for the health assessments of the students and the widows. For this particular population of people, the majority could not afford any kind of health care and would not go to a doctor unless the situation was truly life threatening. Assisting with basic health care assessments such as blood pressure checks and wound cleaning, coupled with education about disease prevention in this case, would then encourage people to seek medical help in the future. Those involved with this initiative believed that this approach would not create an unhealthy dependency on visitors, but would encourage people to seek medical attention before their cases became too severe for treatment.

Most of the children in Muliro Village had never before seen a doctor of any kind other than a traditional healer, and some suffered severely from jiggers (parasites) in their feet, as well as other conditions related to lack of proper hygiene and regular diets with healthy foods. For the majority of the widows, their diagnoses of hypertension and high blood pressure were mostly direct results of poor diets and stress due to their level of poverty and neglect of medical care. Teaching basic concepts of health was a high priority for the nursing team and became naturally integrated into the assessments of both groups.

During the time the George Fox team was serving at the Kaptama hospital, the students observed and participated in the daily business of the facility. Many people came to the hospital just to be around the White people who had come to serve there. The community members surrounding the hospital were grateful for the relational and spiritual care the entire team brought to the facility. People in this region on Mt. Elgon tend to be very distrustful of medical care in general, and also leery of strangers coming into their communities. The *outsider effect*, as discussed in chapter 6, is very prevalent in this area. Even Kenyans from other tribes and regions are viewed suspiciously until trusted relationships are built. As a result, the majority of the people in the Kaptama area often would first seek the care of a traditional healer before going to a trained nurse or clinic officer. Thus, the relationship-building process with the community members was critical for the George Fox team in order to build the respect and trust which would make it possible for future teams to come and serve in a similar way. The hospital staff were grateful to collaborate with the George Fox team and teach them the various aspects of health care and treatment in rural Kenya, but importantly, the nursing students received vital skills in relationship building with those of another culture, and critical thinking skills when they encountered diseases they had never before seen. Cultural humility was evident in the interactions of the students with patients, clinical staff, and community members. Even though these students were serving the

Kenyans in many practical ways, their overall learning far exceeded what they gave during their time of ministry and that was evident in many ways. First, the students learned to work as a team and trust one another and the Kenyan medical staff as they faced a number of life-threatening cases while at the clinic. One student reflected on one of the cases in a team debrief session, "I thought that it was nice to work together with people at the clinic and learn from them, also."

Relationship building was also evident throughout the trip. Another student wrote in her journal at the end of the stay time at Kaptama, "Can't explain emotions; can't put into words; Sad to be leaving Kaptama because of relationships, not knowing if seeing again." Finally, through the various medical situations the students encountered, they all gained confidence in their own calling as nurses, and each situation revealed how they could adapt and respond in difficult situations while in a totally different culture. Another student articulated the building of confidence in this way: "This trip helped me realize my calling for advanced practice."

This service-learning nursing experience to both of these rural Kenyan villages not only benefitted the students, faculty, and the community, but more importantly fulfilled the teaching of Scripture to meet the needs of the poor, the widows, and the orphans. Psalm 82:3–4 reads:

> Give justice to the weak and the orphan;
> maintain the right of the lowly and the destitute.
> Rescue the weak and the needy;
> deliver them from the hand of the wicked.

The positive results and outcomes from this first trip with nursing students planted the seed for future trips of this kind. A follow-up trip to the Kaptama hospital took place just nine months later with yet another team of nursing students and faculty. This trip was a bit easier in the planning process for Eloise and Stephanie since they were now familiar with the overall operations of the hospital and the roles of each employee. Further, the hospital staff also knew what to expect and how to provide the teaching, learning, and cultural opportunities for the students and their professors. Eloise's connections within the community were now also bearing fruit in many ways. A number of the pastors from the mountain told her they remembered her speaking at the Day of Prayer at Friends Moi High School Kaptama a few years earlier. Others mentioned specific events where they had interacted with Eloise during previous visits, and she was continually amazed at their recollection of such events. Since Eloise was back on Mt. Elgon once again, the girls' high school near the hospital requested she pay them a visit. This school was now in its third year of operation since completely separating from the boys' school across the road. The girls were making remarkable progress in all areas of school life, and the school leadership believed that a visit from Eloise would provide additional encouragement and motivation to both teachers and students. Once the visit was arranged, Eloise asked Becky Smith, one of the nursing students, to accompany her and provide some basic health education to the girls. Harry, a son of the region and local host of Eloise's team, escorted the women to the school and facilitated the interactions with the students seated outside in the field, since the school did not have an indoor gathering place large enough for all of the students. After the formal introductions, Harry introduced Eloise and she shared words of spiritual and academic encouragement to the girls. Becky then gave a basic health talk to the girls and provided opportunities for them to ask her questions about health or life. Harry assisted this interaction with the girls and they readily engaged with Becky. Eloise later described this special experience to others: in what seemed a matter of minutes, Becky gained an immense amount of self-confidence and became a nurse educator right before Eloise's eyes. Becky later recounted the interactions with the girls at the school that day were one of the highlights of the entire trip for her! In just two visits from the George Fox team to the Kaptama hospital, relationships were quickly forming between the two groups, and all participating were the beneficiaries of the collaboration. However, there was still more work to do and God soon gave John another idea, which involved collaborating with Eloise and her colleagues in his home village of Kivagala.

John was born and raised in the village of Kivagala in Vihiga County in Kenya. He lived and worked in Nairobi for over thirty years, and when he was relocated to Kisumu, a town near his Kivagala home, he decided to stay at his residence in Kivagala and commute to Kisumu twenty-five kilometers away. When John moved to stay in his home village, he encountered a large number of idle young people not employed, and others with nothing to do during the school holidays. John witnessed how immorality was going on in the village among the young people due to their lack of focus and direction. John was concerned with these issues and decided to create special activities which would keep these young people busy so they could utilize their wasted energy in a positive way.

John organized a committee from the community and discussed with them the possibility of engaging the young people in sporting activities annually in the months of November and December. John worked closely with all levels of people in the community and together they arranged for a sporting activity. John and the community leaders informed the young people of this new opportunity for their involvement, and asked them to form sports clubs ranging from senior men to younger men and women. Even older women, in their sixties and above, were involved in the games. These sporting activities began in 2006 and have increased in popularity in the years since they started. Many young people have been involved in these sports and the idleness has been greatly reduced. Every end of the year, the community of Kivagala hosts these sporting activities and everybody in the community becomes involved in some way. The activities have drawn many young people from other neighboring communities who have come to participate in these competitions.

During the post-election violence that hit Kenya in 2007–2008, the games at Kivagala saw all young people from the Kivagala community enjoying their sporting activities while the whole country was on fire. All the young people were confined on the fields at Kivagala and enjoyed their activities peacefully and were just hearing from the media how the country was on fire with violence everywhere. What started as an activity to keep young people busy and build their sporting talents saw this effort turn into a peace-making activity. John has used his own resources to ensure these activities continue year after year. John identified himself with the community and together they organized the young people, who have since been growing up with a character worthy of the community's growth. John believes every child has something special to offer to society, and through these sporting activities many young people have been raised up through their education as they have played soccer, netball, volleyball, and other sports.

When Eloise heard from John about these activities which he had kept to himself for over eight years, she discerned the time was right to become involved. John was very careful not to involve anybody from America, fearing his position as Africa Ministries Director would be compromised. John never wanted it to appear as if he was taking advantage of his professional position to influence the friends he had in the U.S. to support this worthy program in the Kivagala village. Because of the long and trusted relationship that existed between Eloise and John, it was easy for him to share with

Eloise what was happening within the village. When Eloise learned about this unique activity occurring yearly at Kivagala, she believed it could potentially be another area in which nursing students might partner together with John and the Kivagala community during the sporting camp at end of December.

Since the nursing student initiative was bearing fruit at Kaptama and Muliro Village, John consulted with Eloise and Stephanie about this new possibility and they agreed to consider this initiative. After discussing all of the logistics, John and Eloise decided the nursing students could provide the first aid care for the players during the tournaments and stay at his home in the Kivagala community. In this way, the entire George Fox team would be fully integrated into the community as they served however they could during the sporting events. This was another natural connection to expand the work in Kivagala Village that John has continued to shepherd through the years as a son of the region.

After the George Fox team had collaborated with the Kivagala community during just one football tournament, the community expressed their gratitude for the assistance the nursing students provided to the players, and also for the positive interactions with community members. The George Fox team visited people in their homes and prayed with them, attended church services, played games with children, and also gave health lessons on brushing teeth and handwashing to the local children. Several days later, the nursing students were delighted to observe children outside of their homes brushing their teeth just as the nursing students had taught them. The entire team left the Kivagala community at the end of their service with full hearts from all of the interactions they had experienced with the people. One such interaction remains etched in the memories of the entire team. One morning before the team left to go out into the community, one of the women pastors from the Friends church came to John's house where the team was staying, to have her blood pressure checked. As she greeted the team, she proceeded to enter into a time of singing and worship, then concluded with praying for the entire group. When she was finished, she was ready to have her blood pressure checked. Several of the team members later recalled, "We were there to minister to the people, but here she came and ministered to us!" That was another meaningful example of humility authentically lived out in service to others.

Gahumbwa Friends Secondary School

What happens when one receives a letter from the government informing him that he has been appointed as chairman of a secondary school in his county? Although this event actually happened to John, it also provided him another opportunity in which to practice the framework of cultural humility, and engage other partners in the process.

Gahumbwa High School is a Quaker school near John's Kivagala home. The school has had many challenges in recent years and has not been in good relationship with the surrounding community due to poor academic performance. The school had a very demoralized staff and hence the students lacked an esteem for learning. The school was like an institution heading toward academic destruction. John has called this path to destruction "academic abortion" of the young people going through this school. Since the situation was so dire, there was nothing the school could to do prove its worthiness in the community. Teachers were disunited, had given up on their teaching, and did not have good relationships with the school principal. The remaining school staff were on their own and hence had no coordination with in the school. Students lived on the school site as if they were in a free area, doing what they wished to do. Discipline was not even visible in the school.

John was surprised one day in March 2016 when he received a letter from the Ministry of Education appointing him as the board chairman of the school. One can only imagine what goes through someone's mind when appointed as the chairman of such a school. The problem was where to begin, since everybody in the school was going their own way and there appeared to be no sanity anywhere in their operations.

John contemplated whether he should refuse or accept that responsibility, which was already full of many challenges. After thinking about the possibility of taking up the position, he accepted the appointment to become the chairman of the Board of Management for Gahumbwa High School. John immediately arranged a visit to the school and when he arrived he found the principal seated in her office with all the windows closed, fearing she might be invaded by the community. They had sent her warnings that she should leave the school because she was not doing enough to improve the academic performance of the students. Parents felt their children were being drained from the knowledge they had and were leaving the school valueless. John talked at length with the principal, who was scared and fearful, and encouraged her to take up her position as the principal and not hide in the office even though everything was a mess.

John talked with the Board of Management and agreed to complete a situational analysis of the school before they proceeded with any plans. John and a few members of the board met with teachers separately, then alone with the students, and finally with the non-teaching staff. John intently listened to each of these groups to hear and understand what was happening in the school from each side of the team. These listening sessions, which encouraged them to talk and share the issues and challenges, created a good relationship with the teams, and trust started to develop because they saw a difference in how John was handling things. John brought all of the issues to the whole board and together they discussed how to restore order and confidence to the school. The principal was encouraged and shared what the teams in the school had talked about regarding her own weaknesses.

John organized a meeting with teachers and the principal and encouraged them to stand up to their calling as teachers. Despite the fact the school had performed so poorly, John arranged a dinner for the teachers at a restaurant most of them had never visited, and this opened their eyes to realize they were loved and cared for irrespective of their poor performance as teachers. John also arranged for another principal from one of the high-performing schools to come and encourage the teachers that they were capable teachers and could do their best if they worked as a team. The teachers were inspired by her message, and as they went back to school, they were changed people and started looking at the situation differently. Their teaching approach was totally different after that dinner. John never confronted the teachers with the attitude of quarreling or blaming them, but worked on changing the perception they had that they were not loved or cared for by anybody. John demonstrated spiritual humility through addressing the challenges from a collective responsibility and not blaming anybody, not even the principal for her weaknesses. Everybody took the challenge as a team and agreed to work on the issues together. The students began to notice a different attitude from the teachers, who previously were not friendly to them, and the teachers' attitudes and teaching approach started to make a difference in just a short amount of time.

When John visited George Fox University, he shared with Eloise what he was experiencing with the new assignment as the chairman of the board for Gahumbwa High School. Eloise then talked with her colleagues and they agreed they could find a way to work alongside John and see how the school could benefit through staff development.

Eloise had the opportunity to visit Gahumbwa only five months after John's appointment as its chairman. By this time, due to John's initial work, the attitudes of the principal and staff were vastly improved from John's first encounter with the school. John and the principal had agreed Eloise should come and visit the school and meet the faculty. John was already planning ahead that Eloise and colleagues must somehow be involved in the turnaround efforts at the school, and an initial visit would begin the foundational work for the relationship-building process prior to starting any formal initiatives. The needs of the school were urgent, but it was also important not to rush the process and potentially make mistakes.

As with all other school visits Eloise had experienced, John and Eloise first met with the principal in her office according to cultural protocols, and listened to her share both her struggles and hope for the school. The principal then took them on a formal tour of the school, which ended in the teachers' room. The teachers were finishing their tea time, so John took advantage of that break in the school day to greet the teachers and introduce Eloise to the staff. Eloise and John had already discussed potential topics for this brief meeting with the teachers, but John left the final topic for Eloise to decide. Eloise felt led to share with the teachers about the professional responsibility a teacher has to educate the next generation. As Eloise continued to share her passion for education with these teachers, she noted that many of them had picked up a writing utensil from their desks and were quickly writing down notes from her brief message. As John was leading efforts to turn the school around in academic performance and behavior on the part of students and staff, Eloise knew from experience the teachers must be an integral part of the process. Without their buy-in and overall support, any efforts for school improvement would be futile. At the end of Eloise's visit, John promised the teachers he would continue to find ways to support them in their efforts as teachers, most likely with Eloise and a team of colleagues for professional development sessions.

A few days later Gahumbwa hosted their Annual General Meeting, an event for parents to provide reports of school progress and efforts. John, as board chairman, was obligated to attend, and brought Eloise with him to experience yet another cultural aspect of Kenyan school life. Eloise was invited to speak with the parents and encouraged them to support the education of their students and remain involved and participate with the activities at the school. Eloise also highlighted the importance of education for the future of the students, families, and communities. After the formal events of the day, the skies opened with rain as the invited speaker was concluding his words to the school community. As Eloise expressed her regret to the school leaders that the rain had perhaps interrupted the rest of the festivities for the remainder of the day, the members of the community shared the cultural meaning of the rain. They stated that since Eloise was a special guest in attendance, the rain was a symbol that something new was going to happen, and it was a positive sign for the school from that time forth.

As a part of encouraging this school with so few resources, Eloise was able to find a donor who provided laptops for the key personnel of the school. John gave these laptops to the heads of departments and the principal. This effort lifted the esteem of teachers and they exhibited additional confidence in their teaching. Now John and Eloise would need to wait and see how God would direct their steps for further collaboration at Gahumbwa.

8

Lessons Learned, Applications, and Recommendations

THROUGHOUT THIS BOOK, ELOISE and John have shared the stories of their work and how those stories have connected to the framework of cultural humility. As Eloise and John have collaborated on their various projects, they have carefully documented the details of each project or event, discussed the processes and results, and reflected on which improvements or any necessary adjustments might be required. The primary objective of this chapter, then, is to explain specific lessons they have learned, and make recommendations which may assist others who are involved in similar cross-cultural efforts for service-learning or mission work.

As discussed in chapter 6, both Eloise and John are outsiders when it comes to much of the work they undertake in Kenya. Even though John is Kenyan, he has a form of power because of his ministry role as Director of Africa Ministries for Friends United Meeting, his advanced education, his nearly twenty years of experience as a banker in Nairobi, and even because of the region where he was born and raised. As John encounters all classes of people from all tribes in Kenya, cultural humility provides the necessary guidance in every interaction.

Eloise is even more of an outsider in Kenya because of her white skin and privileged American background. Although Eloise is a female and highly educated, even in a patriarchal society such as Kenya she is still respected and often placed high on a pedestal of honor. Eloise finds she must strive even harder within the framework of cultural humility to dismantle that pedestal in order to come alongside the people of Kenya and earn their trust and respect. As Eloise entered her work in Kenya, she learned quickly that she could not make assumptions about the experiences or background knowledge of anyone with whom she was working. The more knowledge she acquired about the people, their background, work, and other details of their lives, the more she was able to make gains with the cross-cultural collaborative initiatives. Since Eloise tries to stay outside of her *comfort zone* while in any learning situation, especially in Kenya, it has been necessary for her to take extra efforts on her part in order to make the connections needed to build trustworthy relationships. As a student of the people and their culture, she continues to learn some basic Swahili, how to read and pronounce key words and phrases, studies the Kenyan education system, visits with and listens to principals and teachers, and drinks many cups of tea and eats meals with the Kenyans. The fruits of these intentional efforts continue to be evident with each visit and have assisted in her own transformation as a leader and educator. The more she has been able to connect with the Kenyans and their culture, the more the relationships have matured and expanded.

One encounter with a young teacher demonstrated the type of respect some of the Kenyans have toward Eloise. As is common with many of her trips, she was visiting one of the Quaker secondary schools with a Kenyan colleague. They had spent most of the morning at the school, engaging in conversation with the principal and several teacher leaders in hopes to encourage them in their work, in addition to visiting classrooms and the rest of the school compound. As Eloise and her colleague were preparing to leave, the principal decided that one of the young teachers who had participated in the morning meetings would drive the visitors to their next appointment at a school just a few kilometers up the road. Eloise and her colleague settled into the cramped quarters of the small pickup truck, while this young teacher started the vehicle, attempted to engage the clutch, and shift into drive so they could depart on time. Eloise recalls the young man was very nervous as he drove them up the bumpy road, weaving around trying to avoid as many potholes as possible, which had filled with water from a recent rainstorm. Eloise was thinking this was just another common occurrence of life in Kenya, but was also grateful when they arrived safely at the next location. They all exchanged formal goodbyes and the young teacher drove off back to his school. A few months later, Eloise received an email from this young teacher, which further explained his nervousness, but also helped Eloise understand that particular community's view of her. The teacher explained in his email:

Hi, this is the teacher who drove you to Wangulu in western Kenya, when you were on an evaluation tour of the peace education. Am sorry when I drove you to that that school, I was not the best driver I have ever been. I realized that I was tense because of the caliber of people I was carrying. I was imagining that in case anything happened to you, a professor from U.S.A, I would not only be answerable to my government but to the international community as well. You will note that I was tense and would not put the right pressure on the gas and breaks. forgive me for my naivety. Anyway, after that confession, I feel relieved.

The revelation from this young teacher helped Eloise to further her understanding of how others in Kenya perceive her, which in turn she uses to help people realize that she is really just a person, created by God, and equal with them in God's eyes.

How then must we act and respond in order to benefit others? Humility is key in how one engages with others, whether in one's own culture or another culture. Scripture passages such Philippians 2:3 and Romans 15:1–3, among others, exhort the believer to consider others more important than oneself, and also to build up one's neighbor. Eloise and John's primary goals are to come alongside those in need spiritually, emotionally, and physically in ways that honor the other person, which then takes the focus off of themselves and any preconceived personal agendas others may believe they might have. Cultural humility, then, is one way in which anyone can utilize the principles of Scripture regarding humility and work with those from all walks of life and from all over the world.

Humility is not a natural emotion one is born with. Eric Jensen writes that we are only born with the following emotions: "joy, anger, surprise, disgust, sadness, and fear."[1] Therefore, humility needs to be learned since it is not innate in our human character. As a believer becomes more Christlike, humility should be a visible outcome. Eloise describes an example of the visible outcome of humility from her work with the women's group in Muliro Village. During one of Eloise's visits to the village, the women requested that she teach the group a lesson on leadership. Eloise chose to prepare a lesson on servant leadership for the women, one in a series she developed specifically for this group. At one point in the middle of the lesson, Eloise asked the women to consider someone they viewed as humble they could use as an example for how they should live their lives. Eloise

---

1. Jensen, *Teaching with Poverty in Mind*, 19.

initially asked the women not to name anyone in the room, but to think of someone else in their circle of friends or family, leaders in the community, or other acquaintances. After a time of silence, Eloise asked the women if they could provide an example of someone with the qualities of humility and why they selected that person. Again, silence filled the room. Finally, Janet, one of the leaders of the group, broke the silence, spoke up, and said, "Professor, you asked us not to name someone in the room, but you are the example of humility that we look to. You have accepted us for who we are and what we are. You are our example." It was a truly humbling and profound moment for Eloise as she realized the significance of Janet's words and how she had been carefully watched by these Kenyan women. It was also an interesting dynamic of how Scripture teaches us to demonstrate humility, but for Eloise in this case, it seemed awkward when it was pointed out as a part of her character. The lesson here is that people are observing our actions all of the time no matter what the cultural setting.

Even though Eloise and John consistently try to utilize the guiding principles of cultural humility throughout their work, it is in no way a set model that one can use in one setting then take the exact same model to be used in another context. Every situation is different, and it is important to acknowledge such differences from the beginning and not assume that any processes will be the same. Corbett and Fikkert also articulate this belief in their book, *When Helping Hurts*. They state, "There is not a 'one-size-fits-all' level of participation that is best for all churches, missionaries, in all settings."[2] John and Eloise could not agree more.

Eloise shared an example of one such perspective she encountered during her travels. As Eloise was visiting another non-profit organization during one of her Kenya visits, she engaged in conversation with another visitor to the same organization. As the conversation progressed, this particular American businessman grew very interested in Eloise's work with the education initiatives and nursing student trips, and inquired about the model she was using. Eloise explained the framework of cultural humility and the main tenets, but the man kept insisting he wanted know the specific model Eloise was using for her work. Eloise continued to share with him cultural humility presents a type of framework of guiding principles, but following a set model could become too rigid and not allow for flexibility or adaptations to different or unique situations. He did not seem to grasp

---

2. Corbett and Fikkert, *When Helping Hurts*, 149.

Eloise's explanation of cultural humility, and when he did not receive an answer that suited him, their conversation finally led to other topics.

Working with those of other cultures does not mean we need to cross international borders. Cultural humility can apply in almost any setting anywhere in the world. As a practical example, Eloise has been able to apply the concepts of cultural humility within her work in the university, and with other stakeholders associated with her educational role. Different departments across campus may have their own unique cultures, despite residing within the same university at the same location.

Mistakes Will Happen

As one enters into service or mission work no matter where it may be, one is bound to make mistakes. It should just be expected. Mistakes should be viewed as learning opportunities so they become uncommon instead of the norm. However, it is important to remember that within the framework of cultural humility is the posture of putting the other person first. Responses to any kind of mistake or conflict need to reflect a humble spirit and attitude in order to preserve the relationship while working through any misunderstandings or conflicts.

Eloise recounts one small but humorous mistake that involved thirty pounds of buttons. Yes, thirty pounds! Before Eloise returned to Kenya to follow up with the work in Muliro Village, she asked Rose what the women's group needed. Rose responded that the women needed buttons for their sewing projects and to replace missing buttons. The request for buttons seemed reasonable, so Eloise told her supporters buttons were needed for the women of the village. People from Eloise's church eagerly supplied buttons, as did the team members she was bringing along on the next trip. In a matter of a few weeks, buttons of all shapes and sizes seemed to appear out of nowhere, and the team members packed the donated buttons into all pieces of their luggage.

When Eloise and her team arrived to the Muhanji farm, they sorted out the supplies they had brought along, including all of the buttons. Soon they had filled a large box full of the buttons so heavy that nobody could carry it—they had to pull it along the floor! Rose was surprised at the number of buttons but seemed pleased nonetheless. When the women's group arrived for their meeting with Eloise and her team, the women were all given the opportunity to select a small bag full of buttons. However, once the women gathered their supply of buttons, it seemed as if none had been removed from the box. Rose assured everyone she would distribute the buttons to various tailor shops in the area and let others know she had buttons on hand for various clothing repairs.

Several years later, Rose still had half a box of buttons left stored in the corner of one of their bedrooms. As Eloise and Rose discussed this issue later, they realized they both should have been more specific in the request for buttons. Eloise was intentional about asking what the women needed and proceeded to gather buttons, but she should have clarified as to how many buttons Rose needed for the women. Rose had no idea how generous Eloise's friends would be with the request for buttons, so Rose learned to be more specific in her request for certain items. Both women can laugh about this example now, even the team members who once in a while still find a stray button from that trip to Kenya!

Eloise and John have made mistakes in their work and will most likely make some more, but with God's grace they will continue to serve him for the benefit of the kingdom and learn from those mistakes. It is also important not to become so fearful of making mistakes that one becomes paralyzed to the point of not wanting to engage in service or mission work at all. That is not a healthy perspective and could very well limit the way one could be a blessing to others and also limit how God could bless each of us through our service to him.

During one of Eloise's trips with educators, she witnessed a cultural mistake that potentially could have damaged the relationship with the participants of a teachers' workshop. One of the team members, Gloria (name changed), was delivering a lesson on effective methods for teaching argumentative writing. As the lesson was flowing along, Gloria decided at the spur of the moment to interject some examples that might be helpful for the participants as they were preparing their own examples for practicing the concept. For some reason, Gloria chose the topic of arranged marriages and why one would want to argue against arranged marriages. Eloise remembers becoming shocked and wide-eyed with concern as Gloria kept pursuing this topic, not realizing that arranged marriages were still practiced within the community they were visiting. After the lesson when the participants were in their groups practicing the writing concepts Gloria had taught them, Eloise and another team member pulled Gloria aside and shared with her the cultural faux pas regarding arranged marriages. Gloria was absolutely mortified as she realized her cultural mistake, obviously not intended, but while innocently trying to make a specific cultural connection with the participants. Eloise and the team members huddled together to discern how they could recover from the mistake without damaging any relationships. They decided once the participants were finished with their work and ready for the next steps in the lesson, Gloria would apologize for her mistake. That is exactly what she did. Her apology was so thoughtful and authentic the participants took it all in stride and assured her no harm and been done and nobody was offended. In fact, laughter ensued, and a healthy and insightful conversation about cultural practices followed. The Americans and the Kenyans learned more about each other after that mistake than perhaps they would have learned if it had not happened. In addition, that mistake and apology seemed to break the ice even further between the Kenyan participants and Eloise's team as the conversations and relationship building continued during tea times, in the school yard, and out in the community. The important lesson with this example was that even though it was an innocent mistake, there was an immediate apology and an acknowledgement that this team member did not have all of the cultural information before making an assumption about a cultural practice.

John recounted one of his own cultural mistakes involving a female guest from the U.S. One of the leaders from one of the Quaker women's groups in the States came to Kenya to visit various Yearly Meetings and their women's groups. John was excited for her visit and took extra care to be sure all details were in place for her visit. When John and this woman visited the Yearly Meetings, he was the one designated to introduce her to the congregation each time. According to Kenyan customs and culture, he introduced her as "this old lady" from the United States, which was the highest honor of introducing a guest. After a few times she had been introduced in this way, she finally told John she was very offended by the way he had been introducing her. John quickly realized his mistake and asked her forgiveness. John then went on to explain that introducing her in the way he did was actually demonstrating great honor to her as a guest within his culture. However, she did not see it the same way and requested John introduce her in another manner. John humbly obliged and changed his introduction of her for the remainder of her time in Kenya.

Become Informed

No matter what kind of service, mission, or cross-cultural work you believe God is calling you to do, it is vital to become educated and informed about effective practices for this special kind of work. One should never enter into mission or service work blindly, without any kind of a plan or idea of what one will be doing. People may mean well and believe they have good intentions, but those are not enough. Eloise shares one example of an encounter with one such well-meaning person.

As a result of Eloise's frequent trips going back and forth to Kenya, she has had the opportunity to meet some very interesting people, especially in airplanes. One such example was a seatmate on one of her flights. Eloise initiated a conversation with the man, who said he was headed to Kenya for mission work. Eloise explained to him why she was headed to Kenya, and the man became very interested in her work and continued to ask her questions to learn more. After a time, Eloise asked him what he would be doing in Kenya. He explained that he was going to help at an orphanage for a time and then move on to another location in Kenya. The man revealed he had found out about this particular orphanage through another friend and mentioned he planned to leave some money there when he left so that the children could be taken care of properly. This last statement and his lack of clarity about the specifics of what he would be doing was quite concerning for Eloise, so she began to inquire further, while trying not to be too nosey. She asked, "What kind of work will you be doing to help out?" The man was quite surprised at the question and asked Eloise what she meant. She then asked several follow-up questions, including, "How were you connected with the people from that orphanage?" and "Do you have a trusted relationship with the people from that orphanage?" The man replied that he had met a Kenyan somewhere else in his travels who put him in touch with the orphanage. Eloise followed up with another question: "How long have you known this other Kenyan?" The man replied that he was only a casual acquaintance. That response was immediately a red flag for Eloise. As they were nearing their destination and their conversation was coming to a close, she asked the man one more question: "How do you know the money you leave behind will be used as you intend it to be used?" By this time the man clearly was flustered as he had not even considered that possibility or answers to the previous questions, so he asked Eloise what she meant. She explained that without a trusted contact and accountability for gifts or donations, it could be the funds may not be used as he would request.

He was completely surprised at the answer and asked Eloise what recommendation she would have for the money. She suggested he not leave any money this trip but that he begin to build the relationships with the people first, then find out what the children really needed. By the time the flight ended, the man said to Eloise, "I am so glad I was sitting next to you today!" Eloise never knew what happened to the man and his plans while in Kenya, but this encounter was a great reminder of how one must be educated and informed about the best ways to engage in mission or service work, and not take anything for granted. Good intentions have the potential of doing more damage than good if one is not informed or has taken time to fully review the situation.

Eloise and John experienced another example of good intentions after speaking at a conference in the U.S. They had been invited to share their work on cultural humility and presented the main tenets of cultural humility along with specific examples from their work. After the workshop sessions concluded, a man came up to Eloise and John, obviously quite distraught. As he began to share with them, the man revealed he had just come to the realization during the workshop and listening to Eloise and John he had been doing mission work in the wrong way for many years and was deeply remorseful. As Eloise and John continued to listen and then engage in conversation with this man, they encouraged him that God was ultimately responsible for the outcomes, but this was now a perfect opportunity to make the necessary changes in his approach to missions from this time forward using the framework of cultural humility. The man agreed and soon went his way.

It can be too easy to let our emotions overtake common sense and wisdom in our desires to assist with a specific cause or crisis, so that we may unknowingly cause more damage instead of making a positive difference. Cultural humility provides the framework for focusing on the needs of others and carefully discerning the best ways to assist both in the short-term and long-term. It is vital to become informed about best practices of cross-collaborative initiatives and learn what kinds of questions to ask about various projects. Many useful resources are currently available surrounding this topic and Eloise and John are hoping this book will also become one such resource.

The framework of cultural humility can provide reliable guidelines for most service or mission projects most anywhere in the world. Any type of service or mission initiative requires careful consideration for the type of project or activity in which one will engage, as well as any cultural components that need to be considered. As Eloise and John have already discovered, every community is different, even if they are in close proximity, and one cannot expect the same procedures will work from one community to the next, or the outcomes will be similar. This has been true with the nursing program initiative. Even though the medical teams Eloise has brought from George Fox University have worked in several rural areas in different counties, those areas have differed as to the community members' perceptions of health care, the diseases most prevalent, the views about traditional herbal medicine versus modern medicine, and the level of income and what the people could afford for any treatments.

The comparison of the work in Musembe and Kaptama are two such examples of how different communities have responded to cross-collaborative work. Both the Musembe school and the surrounding area of Muliro Village were ripe for harvest, which made the efforts within the community appear relatively easy. The initiative at the Kaptama hospital involving George Fox university nursing students, and more recently the collaboration with a Kenyan physician, has been a totally different story and an example of a program that is taking more time to develop. On the surface it would be too easy for one to become discouraged since it seems the Kaptama community is not accepting or appreciative of the collaborative efforts at the hospital. However, upon further examination of the background of the community, it is more complex than one would be able to observe from the surface level. As stated in chapter 4, the community of Kaptama was deeply entrenched in the violent land clashes of the early 2000's, which resulted in trauma for many of the residents within this region. At one point toward the end of the land clashes, John was involved in trying to broker a peaceful resolution with the warring factions when the government decided enough was enough. The Kenyan military set up a camp in the Kaptama region and bombed the insurgents on the other side of the mountain, in addition to terrorizing the local community. The people from the Kaptama region and other places on the mountain have had little to no support since then to help them recover from their trauma, which makes any kind of change very difficult since they are very leery of trusting people from the outside. However, Eloise and John have seen positive results in a short amount of time, which continues to encourage them to move forward with the efforts at the hospital, schools, and surrounding communities.

Even within the educational communities Eloise and John have worked, they have encountered vast differences not only in the types of schools but in the variance in leadership of the schools, as well as the level of community support. Biases and assumptions must be carefully examined and nothing can be taken for granted in any kind of situation, even with prior knowledge or background. As Eloise and John consider any new initiative in Kenya, they employ several strategies before any work begins. First, they invite people into the process through intentional and focused conversations about the work in Kenya. This is a form of relationship building that is foundational to any cross-cultural effort. Next, they invite people to Kenya to engage with the Kenyans through relationship building, and then carefully discern ways to partner with the work already in process or even begin something new. Visioning and discernment is key so that any collaboration will build up the communities and not promote or cause dependency on Westerners. Once potential partners witness the positive work taking place in Kenya and the many opportunities in which to collaborate, they catch the vision for future projects. Relationship building between outside groups and the Kenyans is central to Eloise and John's objectives.

As one engages in cross-cultural work of any kind, change takes time and may not always be visible, and most assuredly, it just will not happen the way one thinks it needs to happen! One must be prepared to plant the seed or harvest the fruit of the seeds others have planted. God is responsible for the harvest, but we need to be alert as to how God will use us in his efforts. Cultural humility plays a key role in mission and service work as a person or group first waits for God's direction or timing, instead of asserting their own agenda. Even after Eloise and John have engaged in a project for a period of time, they do not keep that project going just for the sake of keeping it going. They are continually and carefully evaluating everything they do in order to be good stewards of their time and God's resources. Further, Eloise and John do not want to encourage dependency on themselves or funding from the U.S., but strive to empower the people they work with so they are able to sustain the project or initiative long after Eloise and John have concluded their part in the work.

Relationship building is an ongoing process. It is not a *once-and-done* effort, especially working with other cultures. An unfortunate practice for some mission or service initiatives is to pop in, complete the project, and leave. That is all, and one can walk away and be done. However, effective cross-cultural collaboration relies on intentional relationship building with others. Eloise and John are still learning how to work with others in meaningful ways that help to empower the others as individuals within their culture, not for John and Eloise's personal gains, but only for the glory of God and his kingdom. Relationship building, setting aside biases and assumptions, intentional listening, and co-learning and collaboration. How might God use you, the reader, through this framework of cultural humility?

Lessons Learned from One Another

Throughout this book, Eloise and John have described their cross-collaborative projects and the various connections to the concepts of cultural humility. But one question might still linger for the reader: What have they learned from each other through all of their work?

One of the key lessons Eloise has learned from John is that relationships with people in Kenya or elsewhere are always priority. In Kenya, it does not matter whether the people are blood relatives, from another family or clan, all are considered family. Often Eloise would become confused when John would call someone a cousin and she would try to clarify exactly how they were a cousin. Clarifying a relationship is uncommon in Kenyan culture because they do not usually assign those types of categories as Westerners typically do. Over the years, John has understood Eloise's questions about family and now will explain whether a person is a blood relative or not. Eloise has learned it does not matter because all are considered family.

In another example of relationships, there have been a number of times when traveling from place to place, John has all of a sudden stopped at a home or business and explained they must pay someone a visit. Eloise has learned not to be upset or annoyed with these occurrences, but rather to view these delays as opportunities to meet new people, and to add to her ongoing learning of cultural practices. At one such time while they were traveling from the farm into Kitale town, John decided to visit the widow of a landholder in western Kenya and check on an agricultural project John and a few other colleagues had recently started. When John and Eloise arrived at the farm, they were ushered into the main parlor of the old colonial-style home and served tea while the elderly widow finished her morning routines in preparation for the day. After Eloise and John waited for over an hour, the widow was assisted into the parlor to meet with them. Due to the language barrier, Eloise could not understand much of the conversation, but the Spirit of God was present as John shared words of Scripture and encouragement with this precious widow. At the end of the visit, John asked Eloise to pray, which she willingly did while John translated. John explained to Eloise afterward, "It was important for her to hear your voice." As Eloise asked for further clarification, John replied that hearing Eloise's voice, even in another language, provides a source of encouragement to people, but especially for this widow who was nearing the end of her days on earth. Unknown to Eloise at the time, this widow had family residing in the U.S. whom Eloise had unknowingly met at a gathering in the States. For this widow, meeting Eloise and hearing her voice provided at least a small connection to these family members whom this widow deeply missed.

Another lesson Eloise has learned from working with John is the passion he so clearly demonstrates to serve not only his people, but others in Africa and beyond. Boundaries do not exist for John in any matter related to spiritual nurturing, leadership, or encouragement. In addition, John very easily adapts to any kind of cultural setting anywhere, thus demonstrating a high level of cultural sensitivity, while practicing the concepts of cultural humility. Eloise and John's collaborative work has included projects in Uganda, Rwanda, as well as in the U.S., and Eloise has observed that John is just at ease in a spacious American home as he is meeting with church leaders in a hut in Uganda. John's attitudes and actions in any kind of situation have provided Eloise with specific examples of how cultural humility can be lived out on a daily basis no matter the context.

In turn, John has also learned much from Eloise in the time they have collaborated together doing their various programs in Kenya. As John has been working with Eloise, he has noted that one can do more with people in the community irrespective of one's education status. According to John, Eloise has modeled one of the highest levels of cultural humility in her work within the Kenyan communities. Her education status has not reduced her from who she is, but she has demonstrated that as one acquires higher education, one needs all the more to come down and build relationship with those who may be considered less knowledgeable or disadvantaged in the community. John believes Eloise demonstrates the ubuntu theology Desmond Tutu wrote about.[3] This is where each of us looks at one other from the belief that we are all equal and created in the same image of God irrespective of our backgrounds. According to John, Kenyan professors never come down to the people, and neither do they mix with different types of people. Kenyan professors are known to interact only with those

3 Haws, "Suffering, Hope and Forgiveness."

they call learned friends. Therefore, others do not make any sense to them at all. Eloise brings a different perspective, as she mingles with all people with or without education. John has learned from her example to be more humble and live together with all in the community.

John has also learned from Eloise how to be patient and take things a little bit at a time. John has been able to learn how to process issues before reacting or giving an answer. According to John, Eloise's cultural humility speaks for itself naturally as she carries out her work among the different cultural communities in Kenya.

Conclusion

Eloise and John have shared narratives of the many projects they have been directly involved with throughout the years. Each project has a special story and meaning for all who have been involved. Each and every story with its descriptions of processes and interactions is true, with only a few names changed out of necessity. Eloise and John have taken great care to accurately portray all of their experiences and not to embellish anything in order to make a point or boast of their work.

Cultural humility has been the framework for John and Eloise's cross-collaborative ministry and will continue to provide the guiding principles. John and Eloise both fully believe that building relationships, coupled with intentional listening, humility, and collaboration, all truly model how God wants us to enter into any kind of initiative or work wherever he calls us. These principles are not just for ministry work in diverse settings, but are fully applicable in any setting. As Eloise has so clearly learned from John over the years, people matter and come first. Each person has unique gifts and abilities and bears the image of God himself. When one views people in this way, then one can more fully embody the humility Christ himself set as an example for the entire world.

Eloise would be the first one to say she is not the same person since she said yes to God and answered the invitation to participate with the very first project in Kenya, the development of the peace curriculum. In fact, she would probably say she has become more Kenyan in her approach: taking additional time to process things, not rushing into decisions, carefully considering the viewpoints of others, and waiting for God's timing for events. Even if the collaborative work she and John are involved with were to stop at this point, God has provided her with rich experiences she will continue to apply in her professional work and wherever else God may lead her.

Over the years Eloise has also noticed a distinctive change in how John approaches his ministry work. His care and compassion for people continues to increase as he recognizes the urgency for people to come to know Christ and become disciples for the kingdom. Both Eloise and John have experienced how cultural humility has transformed their lives in ways unexpected. This is not to say they are both perfect (just ask their families) or have done everything perfectly throughout their projects. However, God's grace is sufficient enough to cover mistakes and blunders as we all learn how to work with people with a humble attitude and perspective. Intentionally incorporating the tenets of cultural humility into our lives is a choice for each person. As cultural humility becomes a way of living for each one of us, it will continue to both transform and inform how we engage and interact with the people God brings into our lives. John and Eloise cannot think of a better way in which to serve the body of Christ.

9

Epilogue

IN EACH CHAPTER OF this book, Eloise and John have explained how they have entered into their various collaborative projects in Kenya, and how those projects connect with the framework of cultural humility. However, as many of these projects have developed even further, Eloise and John believe it is important to provide updated information which will hopefully be an encouragement to the reader.

Musembe and Muliro Village

At the time this manuscript was scheduled for submission, the efforts in Muliro Village continued to bear fruit as the community has become more actively involved in supporting the school through academic support, as well as basic school supplies. For example, the parents' group recently met together and agreed that the preschool children needed chairs for their classroom. The parents pooled their funds and purchased the needed chairs. Even this example is quite a milestone for the community. Prior to Eloise and John entering into the first attempts at building relationships with the Musembe school, parents, guardians, and the surrounding community refused to provide any support for the school since it was so low academically and in a pitiful state. The result was that the children suffered from neglect. In addition, a minor conflict existed since members of the surrounding community were mostly Quaker, but the school was sponsored by the Pentecostal Assemblies of God denomination. Therefore, the Quakers did not see why they should support a school that was not their own. However, as the various initiatives began to bear fruit, the community took notice and parents began to send their children to Musembe once again, and also offer what little financial support they were able to provide. Once the parents witnessed what they were able to accomplish together even when each could only give a small amount, the results have been astounding. In response to the positive changes at the school, one of teachers at Musembe mentioned to Eloise, "Musembe used to be known as the rejected stone, but now, because of the support you have been providing, we are now known as the cornerstone."

High School Scholarships

At the completion of this manuscript, nine students from Musembe were attending various boarding high schools, all making significant progress academically, emotionally, physically, and spiritually. Prior to 2014, no student from Musembe had ever gone on to high school for further education, thus limiting their chances to move beyond their poverty state. The scholarship program has continued to be an incentive for the students and their families. In fact, the program started to cause a bit of conflict since families from other schools heard about the program and began to send their students to Musembe in hopes of earning one of the scholarships. In order to resolve the conflict, Eloise, Rose, and John put extra requirements on the scholarship program so that it could only be for students who had been at the Musembe school for a minimum of three years. No transfer students would be eligible for this program. It is unfortunate they had to set this limit, but scholarships can only be granted with the resources available and donors who have committed to the program. Eloise, Rose, and John are first committed to the community within Musembe to see how they can assist with improving life for the children and their families. When and if God opens doors beyond the Musembe community, then those same efforts can be expanded to other regions as well.

Through the scholarship program and other initiatives at the school, the academics for both boys and girls have improved so much that they now have strong academic rankings throughout the county as compared with other schools. Government education officials as well as other schools have now taken notice that students from Musembe are indeed capable of meeting the national academic requirements. In just three years of the scholarship program and professional development for teachers, the mean score of the students from Musembe on the national exam has increased by over fifty-two points. At the completion of this manuscript, one of the Musembe boys was producing the highest score ever seen at the school, and ranking number three academically in the entire county. Further, the girls' academic progress continues to make major gains. One of the Musembe girls was number fourteen in the Musembe region when compared with other schools. The class 7 girls have been motivated by the improvements and seven of the top ten students are girls. In class 6 the results are similar, with girls in the top five positions. The attendance records show that in the span of three years for all of these programs, including the sanitary supply initiative, the girls now have fewer absences than before, their academic interest and participation continue to rise, and even more importantly, there were no pregnancies among the class 8 girls at the conclusion of the 2016 school year. According to the teachers, that has never before occurred, and the teachers attribute this fact not only to the scholarship program, but also to the sanitary pad initiative and the life skills mentoring program of the women's group from the village.

Health Improvements

Just as remarkable in the progress of the school was the comparison of the health assessments at the Musembe school after only two visits of nursing students to the community. During the first visit to the school in 2015 as described in chapter 7, the nursing team cleaned the feet of many students who were infected with the parasite known as jiggers. This parasite burrows deeply into the feet and lays eggs in the tissues, which then produces more parasites. If not fully treated, the feet become infected and a person could lose their toes or even their feet. Michael, one of the little boys the team treated during the first visit, had an extreme case of jiggers in both feet which took quite a bit of time for treatment. When the nursing students along with several community members concluded Michael's treatment, he was given medicine for his feet and pain, as well as brand new shoes to wear home. When the next team arrived sixteen months later for another round of health assessments at the school, they found Michael was now a healthy boy and thriving physically. Michael's class teacher explained that when his case was most severe, the parasites were active at night and caused him such pain he could not sleep. Once the jiggers were gone and his infected feet had healed, Michael could finally get the deep refreshing sleep his little body needed for him to grow strong. Even his academic performance and concentration improved because he was not so fatigued during the day. In addition to Michael's report, the team found no case of jiggers in any child, and all of the Musembe children were wearing shoes. The teachers explained Michael's case had been such an example to the community that parents and guardians were ensuring their children were wearing shoes and keeping their feet clean. This example was a victory in many ways, in that as the nursing students came along side of this school and community, the parents and community members responded with the type of actions they were able to do in order to keep their children healthy. The results of the work in the Musembe community up to this point have been very encouraging to all involved.

Mt. Elgon School Progress

When John, Eloise, and her colleagues held the first professional development workshops with all the high school principals on the mountain, it was the initial step in restoring academic improvements and healthier school environments for teachers and students. As they visited individual schools and talked to students, they encouraged a team of teachers and students who were very much discouraged due to the ethnic conflicts on the mountain which had demoralized the learning institutions. As a result, the schools on the mountain were performing very poorly up to that time. However, through the cultural humility approach which John and Eloise infused throughout the workshops, both teachers and students in these schools have been transformed and academic performance has improved. In addition, the positive improvements have created a very high interest in learning for both boys and girls. The schools have had a change of attitude toward life and learning, and have recognized the need to respect each other.

In only three years since the workshops were held with the mountain schools, John, Eloise, and the local leaders can testify that the changes are enormous. For example, Kimobo High School, which was once known as the lowest-performing school, has been the best school on the mountain for two years in a row. When put in practice, the principles of cultural humility transform lives by changing how things are done, while at the same time creating a platform for better performance in the schools. Both Friends Moi High School Kaptama and Kimobo Friends High School have taken the lead to improved performance, even after going through multiple challenges from the ethnic conflicts that rocked the community in the very region where the schools are located. The workshops held on the mountain that Eloise and John organized have produced a transforming impact on the young boys and girls in those schools and other high schools which have since seen peace on the mountain.

Both Eloise and John are grateful for the continued positive results with their projects, and credit God for these outcomes. All of the collaborative mission and service work Eloise and John have been involved with is God's and his alone.

To God be the glory.

Bibliography

Adichie, Chimamanda Ngozi. "The Danger of a Single Story." TEDGlobal, July 2009. http://www.ted.com/talks/chimamanda_adichie_the_danger_of_a_single_story.

Bently, Regina, and Kathy Jo Ellison. "Increasing Cultural Competence in Nursing through International Service-Learning Experiences." *Nurse Educator* 32 (2007) 207–11.

Berg, Bruce Lawrence. *Qualitative Research Methods for the Social Sciences.* 8th ed. Boston: Pearson, 2012.

Brehm, Ward. *White Man Walking: An American Businessman's Spiritual Adventure in Africa.* Minneapolis: Kirk House, 2003.

Cercone, Kathleen. "Characteristics of Adult Learners with Implications for Online Learning Design." *AACE Journal* 16.2 (2008) 137–59.

Chang, E-shien, Melissa Simon, and XinQi Dong. "Integrating Cultural Humility into Health Care Professional Education and Training." *Advances in Health Sciences Education* 17 (2012) 269–278.

Christie, Michael, Michael Carey, Ann Robertson, and Peter Grainger. "Putting Transformational Learning into Practice." *Australian Journal of Adult Learning* 55.1 (2015) 9–30.

Corbett, Steve, and Brian Fikkert. *When Helping Hurts: How to Alleviate Poverty without Hurting the Poor—and Yourself.* Chicago: Moody, 2009.

Creswell, John. *Qualitative Inquiry and Research Design: Choosing among Five Approaches.* 3rd ed. Los Angeles: Sage, 2013.

Dawo, Jane-Irene, and Enose M. W. Simatwa. "Opportunities and Challenges for Mixed Day Secondary School Headteachers in Promoting Girl-Child Education in Kenya: A Case Study of Kisumu Municipality." *Educational Research and Reviews* 5.12 (2010) 730–41.

de Negri, Bérengère, Elizabeth Thomas, and A. Ilinigumugabo. *Empowering Communities: Participatory Techniques for Community-Based Programme Development.* Vol. 1, *Trainer's Manual.* Nairobi: Centre for African Family Studies, in collaboration with Johns Hopkins University Center for Communication Programs and the Academy for Educational Development, 1998.

Doll, Joy, and Keli Mu, Lou Jensen, Julie Offman, and Caroline Goulet. "Transforming Practice: International Service-Learning as Preparation for Entering Health Care." In

Crossing Boundaries: Tension and Transformation in International Service-Learning, edited by Patrick M. Green and Mathew Johnson, 174–89. Sterling, VA: Stylus, 2014.

Earley, P. Christopher, and Soon Ang. *Cultural Intelligence: Individual Interactions Across Cultures*. Stanford: Stanford University Press, 2003.

Elmer, Duane. *Cross-Cultural Servanthood: Serving the World in Christlike Humility*. Downers Grove, IL: InterVarsity, 2006.

Jensen, Eric. *Teaching with Poverty in Mind: What Being Poor Does to Kids' Brains and What Schools Can Do About It*. Alexandria, VA: Association for Supervision and Curriculum Development, 2009.

Hardy, Kenneth V., and Tracey A Laszloffy. "The Cultural Genogram: Key to Training Culturally Competent Family Therapists." *Journal of Marital and Family Therapy* 21.3 (1995) 227–37.

Haws, Charles G. "Suffering, Hope and Forgiveness: The Ubuntu Theology of Desmond Tutu." *Scottish Journal of Theology* 62 (2009) 477–89.

Hockett, Eloise. "Kenya Quaker Secondary School Peace Curriculum Pilot Project: Examining the Role of the Principal in the Successes and Challenges of the Implementation." *Journal of Research on Christian Education* 24.2 (2015) 125–43.

Hockett, Eloise, Linda Samek, and Scot Headley. "Cultural Humility: A Framework for Local and Global Engagement." *ICCTE Journal* 8 (2013). https://icctejournal.org/issues/v8i1/v8i1-hockett-samek-headley/.

Hook, Joshua N. "Engaging Clients with Cultural Humility." *Journal of Psychology and Christianity* 33.3 (2014) 277–80.

Kenya National Bureau of Statistics. *Kenya Demographic and Health Survey 2014*. December 2015. https://dhsprogram.com/pubs/pdf/FR308/FR308.pdf.

Knowles, Malcolm Shepherd, Elwood F. Holton, and Richard A. Swanson. *The Adult Learner: The Definitive Classic in Adult Education and Human Resource Development*. 5th ed. Woburn, MA: Butterworth-Heinemann, 1998.

Kohlbry, Pamela Wolfe. "The Impact of International Service-Learning on Nursing Students' Cultural Competency." *Journal of Nursing Scholarship* 48.3 (2016) 303–11.

Kroeber, Alfred Louis, and Clyde Kluckhohn. *Culture: A Critical Review of Concepts and Definitions*. Papers of the Peabody Museum of American Archeology and Ethnology 47.1. Cambridge, MA: Peabody Museum, 1952.

Larrivee, Barbara. "Transforming Teaching Practice: Becoming the Critically Reflective Teacher." *Reflective Practice* 1.3 (2000) 293–307.

Lingenfelter, Sherwood G., and Marvin Keene Mayers. *Ministering Cross-Culturally: An Incarnational Model for Personal Relationships*. 2nd ed. Grand Rapids: Baker Academic, 2003.

Livermore, David A. *Serving with Eyes Wide Open: Doing Short-Term Missions with Cultural Intelligence*. Grand Rapids: Baker, 2012.

Lloyd, Cynthia B., with Juliet Young. *New Lessons: The Power of Educating Adolescent Girls*. Girls Count series. Population Council and Coalition for Adolescent Girls, 2009. http://www.popcouncil.org/uploads/pdfs/2009PGY_NewLessons.pdf.

Merriam-Webster's Collegiate Dictionary. 11th ed. Springfield, MA: Merriam-Webster, 2003. Also available at http://www.merriam-webster.com.

Mulford, Bill. "Leading Change for Student Achievement." *Journal of Educational Change* 7.1 (2006) 47–58.

"National Goals of Education in Kenya." Kenya Education and Softkenya.com, 2016. http://softkenya.com/education/goals-of-education-in-kenya/.

Ndura-Ouédraogo, Elavie. "Diversity, Oppression, and the Challenging Quest for Sustainable Peace." In *Building Cultures of Peace: Transdisciplinary Voices of Hope and Action,* edited by Elavie Ndura-Ouédraogo and Randall Amster, 184–93. Newcastle: Cambridge Scholars, 2010.

Nelson, Andrea. "Why Knowing How to 'Engage' Cross-Culturally Matters: Kenyan Principals' Experiences in Cross-Cultural Collaboration." EdD diss., George Fox University, 2016. http://digitalcommons.georgefox.edu/edd/72/.

Osterman, Karen F., and Robert B. Kottman. *Reflective Practice for Educators: Improving Schooling Through Professional Development.* Newbury Park, CA: Corwin, 1993.

Ross, Laurie. "Notes from the Field: Learning Cultural Humility Through Critical Incidents and Central Challenges in Community-Based Participatory Research." *Journal of Community Practice* 18 (2010) 315–35.

Sermeno, Selena E. "Building a Case for Cultural Sensitivity Through Personal Storytelling and Interpersonal Dialogue in International Education." *International Schools Journal* 30 (2011) 10–17.

Slimbach, Richard. *Becoming World Wise: A Guide to Global Learning.* Sterling, VA: Stylus, 2010.

Tangney, June Price. "Humility: Theoretical Perspectives, Empirical Findings and Directions for Future Research." *Journal of Social and Clinical Psychology* 19.1 (2000) 70–82.

Tervalon, Melanie, and Jann Murray-García. "Cultural Humility versus Cultural Competence: A Critical Distinction in Defining Physician Training Outcomes in Multicultural Education." *Journal of Health Care for the Poor and Underserved* 9.2 (1998) 117–25.

Thurow, Roger. *The Last Hunger Season : A Year in an African Farm Community on the Brink of Change.* New York : Public Affairs, 2013.

UNESCO Institute for Statistics and UNICEF. *Fixing the Broken Promise of Education for All: Findings from the Global Initiative on Out-of-School Children.* Montrea: UNESCO Institute for Statistics, 2015. http://www.uis.unesco.org/Education/Documents/oosci-global-report-en.pdf.

United Nations. *The Universal Declaration of Human Rights.* Adopted by the UN General Assembly, Paris, December 10, 1948. http://www.un.org/en/universal-declaration-human-rights/

Vella, Jane Kathryn. *Learning to Listen, Learning to Teach: The Power of Dialogue in Educating Adults.* Rev. ed. San Francisco: Jossey-Bass, 2002.

Made in the USA
San Bernardino, CA
05 July 2017